ESCAPE from Dark Places

ESCAPE
from Dark Places

**GUIDEPOSTS TO HOPE IN AN AGE OF
ANXIETY & DEPRESSION**

AMBRA WATKINS

New York

ESCAPE from Dark Places

GUIDEPOSTS TO HOPE IN AN AGE OF ANXIETY & DEPRESSION

Published in New York, New York, by Morgan James Publishing. Morgan James and The Entrepreneurial Publisher are trademarks of Morgan James, LLC.
www.MorganJamesPublishing.com

The Morgan James Speakers Group can bring authors to your live event. For more information or to book an event visit The Morgan James Speakers Group at www.TheMorganJamesSpeakersGroup.com.

bitlit

A **free** eBook edition is available with the purchase of this print book.

CLEARLY PRINT YOUR NAME ABOVE IN UPPER CASE

Instructions to claim your free eBook edition:
1. Download the BitLit app for Android or iOS
2. Write your name in **UPPER CASE** on the line
3. Use the BitLit app to submit a photo
4. Download your eBook to any device

ISBN 978-1-63047-726-4 paperback
ISBN 978-1-63047-726-4 eBook
Library of Congress Control Number:
2015912524

Cover Design by:
Stacey Lane Design, LLC

Interior Design by:
Bonnie Bushman
The Whole Caboodle Graphic Design

Author photo by:
Kristina Lynn
Photography & Design

In an effort to support local communities and raise awareness and funds, Morgan James Publishing donates a percentage of all book sales for the life of each book to Habitat for Humanity Peninsula and Greater Williamsburg.

Get involved today, visit
www.MorganJamesBuilds.com

Habitat for Humanity®
Peninsula and
Greater Williamsburg
Building Partner

For Bryce,
my inspiration

TABLE OF CONTENTS

PREFACE

Suddenly confronted with the reality and pain of my son's anxiety and depression, my instincts and experience kicked in:

- My maternal instincts to nurture and protect
- My propensity to analyze and deconstruct
- My aptitude to manage and execute projects

And I set out determined to do what I do—assess the problem and fix it.

As you might expect, all did not go according to plan. Complex, multifaceted, and devoid of a clear root cause, the project quickly transformed into a journey. It became an endless journey across new terrain where the data is unclear, people and organizations work at cross-purposes, and the path is personal—excruciatingly personal.

It just so happens that I discovered my son was trapped in a dark place when I was experiencing a dark place of my own. It took us more than a year to begin healing and to plan our escapes. Despite a slew of obstacles, we each succeeded, and we have been in pursuit of sustained spiritual and mental health ever since.

Although painstaking and ongoing, our story is a story of triumph, and I wanted to share it. So I planned to write a literary article that would make people stop and think about what it means to be in those dark places and to build relationships and create support systems that are critical to recovery.

The idea was that we would write a section simultaneously without sharing it with one another. The experiment worked. Surprisingly, the two versions moved smoothly in parallel while providing each of our unique perspectives. The article format, I thought, would be artistically moving and persuasive. But the more I researched and wrote, the more my writing took me beyond the scope of a literary magazine and beyond the constraints of my imaginative and (admittedly) overly contrived structure.

Writing, more than anything else (to me anyway), is a process of discovery. During the process of writing *Escape from Dark Places*, I discovered many new truths about myself, about society, and about mental illness. My burden for anxiety-ridden teens and twentysomethings grew as I drew a distinct correlation between the disconnectedness of the human experience in the postmodern world with the millennial cry for meaning and purpose.

At the onset of my journey, I was uninformed and ill-equipped to provide the support my son needed; I felt guilty. I found that mothers are often regarded as part of the anxiety problem and are seldom included as part of the solution. I felt marginalized. But I soon learned that it does not have to be that way.

This book encapsulates my journey to understand young people, to trace the source of their anxiety and depression, and ultimately to establish a framework for taking action. The goal is to empower young people and their parents, grandparents, church leaders, and mentors to engage in effective intergenerational dialogue that will inspire societal and spiritual reconnects, fight indifference, create significance, stop the stigma, and disseminate hope.

ACKNOWLEDGMENTS

I want to thank my sister, Dawn Lindsey, for laboring over every one of the more than 49,000 words in this book with me. She hung in there through the entire painstaking revision and editing process with unwavering positivity and commitment. I also want to thank my family, my husband in particular, for all the patience and support I received over the past few years as I have been increasingly consumed by the creation process. And thank you God for the story of my life and for the ability to share that story. May God use the words in *Escape from Dark Places* to bless the people who read them, and to empower the generations to engage with one another in the kind of dialogue that can profoundly and positively impact how we perceive the world.

PART 1
MY JOURNEY

CHAPTER 1
GRADUATION

Mental pain is less dramatic than physical pain, but it is more common and also more hard to bear. The frequent attempt to conceal mental pain increases the burden: it is easier to say "My tooth is aching" than to say "My heart is broken."

— C.S. Lewis, *The Problem of Pain*

MY PERSPECTIVE

The family flew in from around the country anticipating the quintessential college graduation gala—school colors brightly displayed on caps and gowns, banners and flags; young adults beaming with pride, relief, and measured anticipation; a tossing of tassels followed by an effluence of food, fun, and revelry. While the banners and flags flew high, for our family the spirit of the occasion was laden with sadness and fear.

3

My son Bryce tried to hide his anguish, but the truth was soon exposed. He choked down the moist, white cake layered with raspberry filling and piled high with whipped cream frosting; he failed to engage in the most trivial conversations; and he responded to gifts and well-wishes with cordial yet forced smiles and thank yous. Playful badgering from his pint-sized nephew elicited a swift blow that knocked the little guy firmly to the ground. The simplest tasks, such as going to the bank to close accounts, were met with resistance. The heaviness by which Bryce carried himself made it evident that without help from my husband and me, we would not be flying home any time soon.

Bryce graduated with a 3.5 grade point average, but he was not proud of his accomplishments. His father, who had such high hopes for his promising young son and who had worked hard to give him everything he needed and to pay for his education, was brimming with anger and blinded with disappointment. With no context for understanding the source of Bryce's despair, he lashed out without considering the impact of his harsh words, "Stupid . . . idiot . . . thankless kid . . . ," as Bryce sat despondent in the backseat of the car.

Bryce went out for drinks that night with his brother, so the weight of the situation was temporarily suspended, and we slept. As we drove our oldest son to the airport the following day, he revealed that a few months prior, Bryce had taken a handful of pills in hopes that he would not wake up. My heart sank immediately. I flashed back to those days Bryce and his older sister were in high school when we lived in Virginia. We had bought a big colonial home there so the kids could bring their friends over. Bryce had the entire walkout basement to himself. The desk in his room looked out over the backyard, and the adjoining game room and den with a pool table, an air hockey table, and a big-screen TV led directly outside to the pool. We added a gym, as well, with all the bells and whistles—an exercise machine, a weight bench, dumbbells, foam flooring, mirrors, and another TV.

Bryce stayed downstairs a lot, too much I feared. I knew that he spent much of his time lying on the bed or on the couch, music blaring. But he was doing well at school, and he was playing sports, so what could be wrong? I wondered. We talked about it occasionally. I remember one day in 2007. I was cleaning the garage and stopped to listen to an interview on the radio with Senator Gordon H. Smith. The senator was releasing a book about his twenty-two-year-old son, who had killed himself. I remember him saying that in retrospect, he and his wife could see that there were times when their son had gone to dark places where he could not be reached. Sobbing, I ran downstairs, sat next to Bryce, and asked if he went to those dark places. He told me, "No, Mom," and laughed as if I were being silly. Somewhat relieved, I finished my outdoor chores. *Should I take Bryce to a psychiatrist?* I asked myself. *If I do, will he be labeled? Will it negatively impact his future?* He had assured me he was okay.

The day after graduation, Bryce lay on his bed in the third-story, corner apartment we rented for his junior and senior years at the university. The apartment, replete with furnishings and decor that make for comfortable college living, displayed no signs of plans to vacate. There was much washing, cleaning, and packing to be done, but Bryce could not even lift his head off the pillow to answer my barrage of questions: *What did you just swallow? Are you still taking Adderall? Are you taking other stimulants or antidepressants? Will you try to overdose again?* I called the hospital, and they told me to bring him to the emergency room if I thought he was going to harm himself. But I did not know. And what would they do with him if I brought him in anyway? I called my insurance company to talk to a mental health specialist; the only solution she offered was admittance to a rehabilitation center back home, but I did not even know if he had an addiction. There were questions, questions, and more questions, but no answers. My husband and I washed clothes, cleaned, and packed the cars so we could all go home. I told Bryce that if he wanted our help he would have to hand over all of his medications, but he refused. At that point I knew that the quest for the light at the end of the tunnel, the journey through this uncharted territory, was going to be challenging and treacherous.

BRYCE'S PERSPECTIVE (HIS OWN WORDS)

I had just finished four finals in one day and was walking back to my one-bedroom apartment alone. The sky was pitch-black. Not even the stars wanted to be around me that night. Rain began to fall and blistering winds hit my cheeks—this wasn't in my forecast. At home, the rain hit my windowpane and started to freeze. I filled in the bubbles on the last Scantron I would ever use in my undergraduate career. I had reached the end of the battle, but the war within me wasn't over, and I felt my enemies returning—anxiety and fear. Questions buzzed in my head like flies trying to find a way out of a closed window. Depression gave birth to a swarm of questions: *Did I do everything in my power to have the highest GPA? Are my parents proud of me? Will I be able to stick a perfect landing in the finance industry?* The questions were trapped inside, and I feared they would never be freed.

Friends of all types and colors drained the juice from my iPhone battery. Everyone was going out to party. Drunken voicemails were left as a reminder that this was the moment to celebrate the college season finale. I lay paralyzed in my bed. Depressed. The speeding cars of disappointment crashed into my parents' high expectations of me. The pressure started nine years back when I was at my brother's college graduation. The speakers talked more about the people with gold ribbons than they did about my brother, and I promised my parents then that I would graduate with honors. The broken promise flooded misery into my world, breaking every levee leading to my sanity.

Six frosted cans of Miller Lite pushed 10 milligrams of Valium down my pipe. Nothing happened. My tolerance was dangerously high. Before

I pulled the covers over my head to block the light pouring in through the blinds, one of my best friends appeared on the face of my phone. He told me to join the crew at the bars; everyone was getting shit-faced that night. I had a swanky apartment a few blocks away from the intoxicating action. "I'll be there," I said. I dragged myself from my bed to look at my face in the mirror to be sure it was clear. It wasn't. Then I looked at my hair: it needed to be trimmed. I was torn between facing a crowd of people who would inevitably judge me or staying inside to be safe. I started crying and shaking uncontrollably. I felt hideous. Then my dad called and said he would be picking me up to go with the family to have hibachi at Shōgun, our favorite establishment for celebrations. I was obligated to go but spent most of the night either in the bathroom or with my head down on the table. After that disaster, I took my brother and his girlfriend to Dixon Street to party for a while, and by the time I hit the sheets, I was totally wrecked.

The next morning, I tried to pop my pimples, but it only exacerbated the problem. When I'm aesthetically perfect, I'm Superman. And when I have a blemish on my face, I'm Clark Kent. I was going insane. I couldn't stop picking at my face. The Valium had not taken away my anxiety, so I went to the kitchen to invite another magician to the pity party. I shoved a bottle of Tylenol PM down my throat and felt a hailstorm of pills going down to my stomach. *I don't want to kill myself,* I reflected. *I just want this depression and pain to stop.* I had the chance to swim with all the fish in the sea. Instead, I lay on the beach to let my oily skin absorb the salty tears of the ocean. I rubbed to remove the crust from my eyes. Empty cans surrounded my bed like battleships; the potent enemies were now casualties. But instead of feeling victorious, I had sour breath, a throbbing head, and an insatiable desire for an ocean of filtered water.

It was my graduation day. Tradition sings the same tune in every region of America. Parents come to honor their children who survived the stress of college life. Families gather to commend the graduate on surmounting a hurdle that less than 20 percent of Americans do. I didn't want anyone to honor me though. I didn't deserve to be honored. Furthermore, I didn't deserve to be loved—by anyone. My peers and I would throw the same caps in the sky after commencement, but my sky was not bright and beautiful like their sky. Thoughts of suicide still loomed in my head from the last failed attempt. Society had told me to dedicate myself to a GPA. They told me I would be successful if I had the highest grades in my class. I believed them, so I dedicated myself to that end. They told me that upon graduation I would fly, so why did I feel I was still sitting alone at the starting gate?

I was seated inside the arena at the graduation ceremony. I felt my body start to hunch over like the wings on a bat to prevent anyone from looking at my face. My thoughts flew to a dark cave filled with all my fears and anxieties: my imperfections, my rejections from girls, my GPA, and no job offers. I could hear the faculty and administration preaching the same thing I had heard for years—how successful we are going to be now, how many jobs we would have because of the university's reputation. I was irate. I hated myself for being fooled into believing something so ridiculous.

It was my turn to shake hands with the dean of the business college and to receive my diploma. The exchange was projected on a large screen, displaying my imperfections to all in attendance. Anxiety coursed through my veins as though it had been administered with a needle. I felt like I was swimming in a fishbowl. Everyone could see the flaws on my face. I was a regular Joe, no gold ribbons around my neck. As I trudged across the stage, I could see my family clapping and cheering.

The sun fell then rose again the next day as God intended. I went to bed with high anxiety, and sure enough it was hugging me tightly when I woke up. I had to reach out to someone, and it could only be my brother. He was leaving for the airport in the afternoon, so I built up the courage to ask him a favor over breakfast. I opened up my dirty laundry and told him what I was going through. I still remember his face. It looked as if a Victoria's Secret supermodel had just broken up with him. I struggled to lift my head while I asked, "Can you tell Mom and Dad about how I tried to kill myself?"

I didn't know how to express what I was going through to parents who felt like strangers to me. I knew my brother would be capable of disclosing my mental health succinctly. His diction grips every awkward situation, and his reasoning opens the most sealed shut minds. He gave me a hug, slapped me five, and assured me that he would explain everything to Mom and Dad. A few minutes later my parents showed up. "I want this apartment packed up when we get back from taking your brother to the airport," they said firmly. I shut the door behind them without acknowledging the urgency they tried to instill in me. We had to be ready for our plane ride back to Florida the next day. The walk back to my bed felt like forever. I pulled the sheets over my head to find my comfort zone—escape from the world—and before long my parents returned to the same unpacked apartment. They were bewildered. Why was their newly minted graduate in bed? Their reaction wasn't anger or sadness; they were just confused as to why I wasn't doing the simple and obvious tasks that lay before me. The same question was hurled at my head again and again. I popped an antianxiety pill my friend had traded me for Adderall. I didn't care about hiding it. In a disturbing way, I kind of wanted them to see me take it.

 CHAPTER 2
HEALING

The way you help heal the world is you start with your own family.
— Mother Theresa

FIRST STEPS

Back home, it was just me, Bryce, and Romulus (our English cream golden retriever). Unable to find a good government contracts position nearby, my husband, Steve, was living a few hours north and commuting home on weekends. I took Bryce with me to the beach, where he could feel the warmth of the sun and listen to the waves crash to decompress. This phase of treatment proved successful in that he was able to release some of the pent-up anxiety smoldering at the surface. I knew we had to go much deeper though, and for that we needed help.

I prayed; then I searched the Internet. *Should I use the keyword "depression?" "Anxiety?" "Psychiatrist?" "Psychologist?"* I was not sure, but after many calls, we spoke to a psychiatrist with whom Bryce sensed a connection. On the appointment day, we sat in the small waiting room on the third floor of a nondescript office building. The room, rather grungy, took me back to the '70s with its paneled walls, Early American coffee table, console television, and sagging brown plaid couch. Ten minutes past our appointment time, we were both ready to bolt when the psychiatrist opened the door to the adjoining room, introduced himself using his first name only, and invited us in. As I surveyed the office and observed the doctor in his faded jeans, plaid camp shirt, and unkempt hair, I wondered what I had gotten us into.

The facade, it turns out, was all a part of the psychiatrist's strategy and style, and soon he put us at ease. By the second session, he had diagnosed Bryce with anxiety and obsessive-compulsive disorder (OCD) and initiated a treatment plan that included a low dose of an SSRI (a selective serotonin reuptake inhibitor, which helps the brain maintain an adequate supply of serotonin) and a benzodiazepine (a mild sedative that helps prevent panic attacks), along with weekly talk sessions. Over the course of these sessions, I began to understand how bleak the last few years had been for Bryce and how much strength and courage it must have taken for him to hide his struggles and finish his degree; and Bryce began to understand that there is a healthier way to perceive the world.

Like Bryce, I needed healing. I was staying in an abusive work situation in order to see my sexual harassment claim through to its conclusion. The various means of retaliation I was forced to endure every day left me isolated and frustrated, exacerbating the initially two, and then three herniated disks in my neck. Despite nine months of therapeutic ultrasound, spinal decompression, and electrical muscle stimulation, my spasms had not relented. Trips to the ER had become more frequent, and I was running out of options. Desperate, I appealed to my chiropractor, who coordinated with my neurologist, a physical therapist, and a pain management facility to establish a holistic treatment plan, and I took FMLA leave.

I checked on Bryce when I was not at the doctor, resting, or otherwise absorbed with documenting my case. Sometimes Bryce checked on me when I was having a bad day; he brought me food or medication and asked if I needed to be taken to the ER. His condition, however, left him predictably self-absorbed. He found it difficult to get up in the morning. When he did get up, he usually looked at himself in the mirror and then retreated back under the covers. Sometimes he came to me sobbing uncontrollably in the midst of what I came to realize was an anxiety attack. I encouraged him to go to the gym with me so that he could release some of the emotion. After a few workout sessions, he picked up a girl, a habit he had fallen into during college to satisfy his need for validation. She was in her mid-twenties, although she looked much older. A hairstylist by trade, she lived with her mother and spent all of her spare time at the gym. Her narcissism fed Bryce's OCD obsession with his looks.

We each had our personal battles to fight, and we often irritated and angered one another. But when in those dark places where we could only go alone, knowing that someone close by recognized the struggle and cared seemed to prevent the darkness from totally obscuring the distant light.

NEW BEGINNINGS

Government contracts were drying up, and the pipeline did not look promising for Steve's employer; however, he was offered a consulting position in Canada. So after much prayer and deliberation, we decided to start yet another chapter in our lives. He would be working a rotation—twenty days on, ten days off. We could stay in Florida, but the commute would be horrendous. Bryce had a job interview in Denver, and my sister lived there, so that was another option. My daughter had moved to Florida from Arkansas with her husband and son, as a series of bad decisions over the course of four years had left them with no options but to reach out for our help. Still estranged from her brothers, my daughter and family were living with Steve; but now that we were considering Denver, my sister and her husband decided to take a chance and offer my son-in-law a job. Denver was a direct, two-and-a-half hour flight from Saskatoon, Canada, so the Rocky Mountains seemed like the right choice.

Bryce was showing signs of progress in his therapy sessions. At least he was beginning to realize how irrational his thought processes could be. He accepted the irrationality of thinking that his skin had to be flawless or no one would want to be around him, for example. Or the irrationality of considering himself a nobody, yet feeling everyone is looking at him, judging him. Or believing his parents and society make unreasonable demands on him that he cannot possibly meet. The gradual process of introducing the medication had barely begun; he was at 2 cc of fluoxetine, a fraction of what the psychiatrist projected would increase to 60 mg of Prozac. I recognized Bryce's condition was still unstable, and his tendencies to self-medicate posed a risk, but he was making progress. After much soul searching, I determined that transitioning to a new location would best accommodate everyone's needs. Bryce headed to DC to visit his brother. Then he was off to Denver where he would stay with my sister until I found us a new place to live. Eager to get her husband working, my daughter packed up her car and headed west too. I had completed the mediation hearing and had a termination date. I was doing physical therapy at home for my neck and was taking a few medications to manage the pain. Now all I had to do was relocate three cars, two households full of furniture, and one golden retriever 2,000 miles across the United States.

We all met up in Denver on Friday, May 3. Steve and my daughter picked me up at the airport, and we all picked Romulus up when he finally arrived. The furniture, en route via Pods, was to go directly into storage, and the cars were to arrive on separate transports in the upcoming weeks. Steve and I felt some relief and were happy to be together. The next morning we were enjoying our coffee and morning walk with Romulus, formulating a strategy for finding a new home, when my father-in-law called. Steve's mother had died suddenly that morning as a result of an apparent heart attack, though we conjectured it had more to do with her lungs and a blood clot in her leg related to a botched medical procedure and a series of painful laser treatments intended to correct the damage. Devastated, we quickly shopped for appropriate clothing (as all our Sunday best was elsewhere), and my sister prepared her Mercedes-Benz Sprinter for immediate departure. Grief rushed in upon the anxiety and stress of the past weeks and months, but nothing was more important at that time than honoring Steve's mother and supporting the family. Exhausted, we arrived back in Denver just in time to help my daughter find an apartment.

My sister had been previewing homes for me while I was still in Florida, using FaceTime to take me on virtual tours. The housing market was still out of whack; there was very little inventory, and when a home did pop up, it was under contract within a matter of days. Competing bids were exceeding the asking price, just like when we bought the house in Virginia right before the bubble burst in 2007. We viewed a home the day we got back from Arkansas, the day it went on the market in a city called Lone Tree, located just south of Denver. It was convenient to shopping, the rail system, downtown, the airport (essentially everything we needed), and when we walked in the front door I whispered, "I love it." We made one of five offers that weekend, and thanks to some good advice from our realtor, we came out on top. Closing was scheduled for June 6.

Steve drove to Canada, and I moved into my sister's house, where she lives with her husband and four children. Bryce occupied the guest room in the basement, and one of the children offered to share with a sibling so I could have a room to myself too. When he must, Bryce can put on a convincing persona, making an appearance and interacting just enough to seem as though he is fine, and then retreating to his room. So the arrangement worked. To Bryce's credit, he also managed to search for jobs and attend interviews.

As the house closing process commenced, I helped out with my nieces and nephew as best I could and attended to other details surrounding the move. In the meantime, my sisters and I planned my dad's eightieth birthday party, which took place in Houston in June. Bryce felt as though he needed to focus on the job search, so he did not attend. But before we returned, he secured a temporary position with a real estate investment firm and started working. Although he was able to get up in the morning, drive himself to the rail station, work, and then reverse that process, he was mentally and physically drained by the week's end and spent most of the weekend sleeping. It was not long after I moved into our new home that Bryce decided to join me and occupy the lower level.

Bryce was still in the process of slowly increasing the level of Prozac intake under the occasional and remote supervision of his psychiatrist in Florida. Despite the doctor's recommendation against it and my outspoken disapproval, Bryce soon chose to add Adderall back into the antidepressant/sedative mix. I grew increasingly concerned about the impact this drug combination was having on his psyche. First the Adderall would bring him up in the morning; then the sedative would bring him back down at night to increase the remote chance of being able to sleep, while the Prozac was taken in an effort to combat the anxiety throughout the course of the day. He often seemed motivated and engaged but could easily slip into a state of passivity. Unexpectedly he would grow depressed and stealthily retreat into his room. We had to find help in our new environment despite the fact that 1) it would be difficult for Bryce to leave work for recurring appointments, and 2) Bryce was determined to manage his own prescription intake. I searched long and hard for a psychiatrist in the Denver area who would have talk therapy sessions with Bryce and could prescribe medication as well. The practice, it seems, is not common here, but eventually I found a doctor who would see him and accept insurance. I attended the first session with Bryce but was quickly made aware that she did not do what she called "family therapy," so Bryce was on his own.

While he was on his own in therapy, I was still available to listen and respond to his complaints and musings, mostly about the human condition and corporate life in America: *How can you act ethically when your peers and superiors do not? How can you react like a Christian when everyone around you is acting out of self-interest? How are people who do not know how to do their jobs able to assume leadership positions? How can a young person ever get ahead?* While all these questions are reasonable, I never knew what to expect from day to day.

Sometimes we enjoyed a logical discussion about work ethic, for example, or about a sermon delivered by our favorite pastor that we streamed on Apple TV. At other times the discussions were contentious. On those days, the arguments could go on for hours and would typically end abruptly in a frenzied fit of anger. "You don't understand. You never went through what I'm going through," he would say. When, in fact, his dad and I had struggled many times, and he knew that to be true. Or, he would argue, ironically, that we had given him everything. We never forced him to struggle, so how was he supposed to know how to grow up? I had been left out of therapy—marginalized. Now Bryce expected me to provide support on an as-needed basis, even though I was ill-equipped. Several days would pass before we would speak again, allowing us time to stop and reflect, allowing *both of us* time to stop and reflect.

Hopefully he would internalize some of the truths I tried to consistently communicate, and I would be able to process the conversation from his point of view.

Most people who have worked in the corporate world know the toll the culture can take on your confidence and self-esteem. But as a millennial straight out of college, Bryce was wielded quite a blow. He was devastated, for example, when in an after-hours social setting a colleague debased him for his youth and good looks. People do this, we know, to boost their own self-image, but for Bryce (as for any fragile, young employee new to the workplace) the bluntness of the words and the ease by which the words were uttered were crushing. Bryce quickly learned another hard lesson. It is a widely known fact that millennials feel they are entitled to express their opinion to anyone at any time, even if that means telling CEOs where they have gone wrong. While Bryce did not meet with the CEO, he did make it clear to his immediate supervisors that the processes the company used to conduct business, particularly in terms of communication, were both ineffective and inefficient. Needless to say, he was not one of the temporary employees asked to continue their employment. He had learned his first lesson in office politics.

It was not long, however, before Bryce found another job at a large Fortune 100 company. Most days he did not want to be there, as he would prefer to manage his own investment firm. And while he could not yet see the path to success in the complex and cutthroat world of finance, nor recognize how long it typically takes to get there (he has always wanted to be a CEO yesterday and believes he deserves to be one today), he was getting out of bed every weekday, going to work, and fighting the battles, regardless of how his skin looked.

Although Bryce could still be short-tempered and irrational, the explosive incidents became less frequent. While it did not come naturally, I consciously made decisions to address fewer of his physical needs, making living at home less convenient and comfortable, which

I hoped would persuade Bryce to make living independently a short-term goal. I knew leaving well enough alone would have been easier because by taking action (or choosing not to take action) I risked provoking a confrontation. But both of us knew he needed to grow up—for his own sake.

Around the October timeframe, Bryce had written off all women as more trouble than they are worth and determined that moving forward, he would focus only on his career. Not many weeks later, however, an old flame rekindled, and he began to get a taste of what it is like to share your life with someone you love. In a matter of weeks, she had moved to Denver, they were engaged to be married, and they had moved in together. Though he was overjoyed, the emotional and financial pressures took a toll on him. He was quick to stand up and own responsibilities relative to his commitment (car insurance, phone bills, and the like), but as if in a pressure cooker, the intensity of his personality began to heat up again followed by more exhaustion and a need for an exorbitant amount of sleep (a side effect of the stress, the medication, and the combination of medication and alcohol).

In spite of all the challenges and unknowns, I believe Bryce's traditional Christian beliefs and values are what grounded him during that first year of healing. Rising each new day knowing that God is sufficient and unchanging gave him hope. As he said on graduation day, "The sun fell then rose again the next day as God intended."

CHAPTER 3
NAVIGATING

And yet for all the advances brought by the study of neurochemistry and neuroanatomy, my own experience suggests that the psychological field remains riven by disputes over what causes anxiety and how to treat it. The psychopharmacologists and psychiatrists I've consulted tell me that drugs are a treatment for my anxiety; the cognitive-behavioral therapists I've consulted sometimes tell me that drugs are partly a cause of it.

— Scott Stossel, *My Age of Anxiety*

Despite the diagnosis and prescriptions, the struggles remained. My search for answers first led me to the field of psychiatry, but the path ahead was still not clear; so my search continued. Bryce is a big Stephen Colbert fan, so sometimes we watched recordings of *The Colbert Report*. There I saw an interview with

Scott Stossel. Maybe someone who actually lives with anxiety could help me find my way, so I read his book. In *My Age of Anxiety: Fear, Hope, Dread, and the Search for Peace of Mind*, Stossel demonstrates that the causes of anxiety disorders (which include OCD) are still widely debated. Biological? Emotional? Physiological? Philosophical? Spiritual? Cultural? No root cause has been ruled out. The earliest extant anxiety-related writings are from the fourth century Greek physician Hippocrates, founder of medicine as a rational science and author of the Hippocratic oath. Robert Burton (1621) documents Hippocrates's description of one patient's symptoms: "He dare not come into company for fear he should be misused, disgraced, overshoot himself in gestures or speeches, or be sick; he thinks every man observeth him."[1] Beyond that brief description, medical science was virtually silent on the subject until Kierkegaard and Freud put pen to paper in 1844 and 1920, respectively.

As late as 1947, there were only three academic papers published on anxiety. In fact, anxiety did not exist as a diagnostic category until it was introduced into the third edition of the American Psychiatric Association's *Diagnostic and Statistical Manual of Mental Disorders* (1980). Not long after the publication of that edition of the manual, pharmaceutical companies were designing drugs to treat the new disorder. And by 1999, Paxil was FDA approved and on the market, supported by a multimillion-dollar-marketing campaign that targeted patients and their physicians. Interestingly, within the approximately twenty years between the categorization of anxiety as a disease and the initial go-to-market of antianxiety drugs, the number of diagnoses escalated from minuscule to approximately twenty million.[2] By 2008, there were more than twenty antianxiety drugs on the market, and despite being some of the most addictive, mind-altering drugs in the world, drug providers filled eighty-five million prescriptions for the top twenty drugs alone.[3]

While the number of patients, academic papers and conferences, treatments, and drugs are now plentiful, for those who suffer from anxiety, managing the disorder is still a crapshoot. Stossel, himself a victim of multiple anxiety disorders and phobias, writes:

Here's what I've tried: individual psychotherapy (three decades of it), family therapy, group therapy, cognitive-behavioral therapy (CBT), rational emotive therapy (RET), acceptance and commitment therapy (ACT), hypnosis, meditation, role-playing, interoceptive exposure therapy, in vivo exposure therapy, supportive-expressive therapy, eye movement desensitization and reprocessing (EMDR), self-help workbooks, massage therapy, prayer, acupuncture, yoga, Stoic philosophy, and audiotapes I ordered off a late-night TV infomercial.

And medication. Lots of medication. Thorazine. Imipramine. Desipramine. Chlorpheniramine. Nardil. BuSpar. Prozac. Zoloft. Paxil. Wellbutrin. Effexor. Celexa. Lexapro. Cymbalta. Luvox. Trazodone. Levoxyl. Propranolol. Tranxene. Serax. Centrax. St. John's wort. Zolpidem. Valium. Librium. Ativan. Xanax. Klonopin.

Also: beer, wine, gin, bourbon, vodka, and scotch.

Here's what's worked: nothing.[4]

Some drugs helped for a short period of time, Stossel admits, but nothing has relieved the underlying anxiety that makes his life a misery. Even at age forty-five, when he knows he will be facing a situation that triggers his symptoms, he continues to experiment with various types and dosages of drugs, typically mixing them with alcohol, with limited success and repeated failure.

In my search for the best way to navigate by exploring the life of someone who suffers from mental illness, I came to the realization that psychiatry is a science that is still young and evolving and that sometimes medication causes more problems than it fixes. More importantly, what I learned was that you can choose the path like Stossel chose, whereby you can let your illness define you, but that is the path to self-perpetuating despair. I also came face-to-face with the reality of the limited development in the field of psychology, particularly as it relates to anxiety disorders. Our initial sessions with the psychiatrist in Florida seemed fruitful; in my naiveté I thought we were on a path that would sustain us until Bryce could wean himself off of the prescribed medications, at which point normal life as we knew it would resume. I had been mistaken.

The first psychiatrist in Florida was a good start. He offered the diagnosis (which I tend to think is fairly accurate), he connected with Bryce, and he responded promptly to all our texts and calls. It became increasingly clear, however, that should Bryce not agree to certain conditions, the psychiatrist would no longer treat him. Bryce, who had recently turned twenty-one, would be required to refrain from consuming any alcohol, not even one beer or glass of wine. He would not be able to take the Adderall his body had grown accustomed to (since that is not one of the drugs in this psychiatrist's repertoire), and if Bryce preferred cognitive therapy, he should curtail the current treatment plan and go see a psychologist who offered that option. Although this psychiatrist took my insurance, it was out-of-network and had to be paid at the time of service via check or cash.

The second doctor in Denver, listed under "Find a Psychiatrist" on the Internet as having an RN, CNS, PNHNP, CACIII, LPC, (looks impressive) but not an MD, concurred with the initial diagnosis and continued treatment with similar drugs at increasingly higher dosages. She was amenable to adding Adderall into the mix, which Bryce felt he still needed. However, she did not immediately connect with Bryce, and she discouraged my attending his sessions because she "doesn't do family therapy." But she took my insurance, so we thought we could make it work. Then, after six months or so of treatment, when I noticed Bryce's behavior deteriorating, I reached out to her via email:

Hi XXXXXX,

I have some concerns about Bryce, and while I understand Dr./ patient confidentiality, the nature of my concerns are such that I hope you can provide some guidance.

Bryce is under additional stress now that he is engaged. Plus, he is under a deadline to find an apartment, as the lease at the place where they are living is running out and it's too far from work to continue living there. (Then there is the fact that he is constantly worrying about where he will be five years from now in his career and financial status.) At the same time, he has cut back to 40 Mg of his medication, despite my efforts to make sure he involves you in prescription decisions. Of course he thinks he knows better how he feels, he believes you don't care, and he feels financially constrained.

The result is he is behaving badly. He is walking around in a continuous rage, treating his fiancé and me with a great deal of disrespect—he's downright mean. I suspect that his behavior carries into the work environment as well. That means that if he continues down this path he will lose the woman he loves and perhaps even his job. And because he is a grown man, I can no longer pick up all the pieces.

I would appreciate your professional opinion as to how I can get Bryce back in to see you so you can better assess the situation and provide him with the medical advice he requires.

Regards,

Ambra

Here is her callous reply:

Hi Ambra,

I have no magic to offer about getting Bryce in to see me other than to tell him what you are seeing. He will know anyway because I need to copy him on this email.

XXXXXXX, RN CNS MA PMHNP CACIII LPC

I was mortified. Should Bryce decide to sever all ties with me, it would be understandable, but it would be risky to eliminate a key person from his support system. Even worse, depending on his current state of mind, information like this could cause him to take some drastic action, like attempt suicide again. All I could do was hope that Bryce would overlook the email in his inbox, but he did not. Fortunately, however, he knew in his heart of hearts that the email was sent out of love and concern for his well-being, so we reconciled. He informed me that he was now taking his medication based solely on how it made him feel, and he was trying to wean himself off of Xanax. (*Maybe he can,* I thought. *After all, I have been able to wean myself off of pain medication by removing myself from an environment riddled with negative stress, managing other sources of stress, increasing the amount of my daily exercise, and improving my eating habits.*) So I repeated my "do not self-medicate" lecture, insisting that he manage all his medication under a doctor's supervision; then the search for yet another psychiatrist began.

I pored through pages and pages of listings for psychiatrists in and around the city and was discouraged to find that only one accepted Bryce's insurance plan, but the office was far from his job, making it impossible to manage. He decided instead to see a general practitioner. It turns out that he liked this doctor and that he had a connection with her, primarily because her own children take medication for anxiety, but little to no progress was made in terms of adjusting medication. She switched him to a new anxiety medication called BuSpar, after which he spent several weeks walking around in a rage. After blowing up at the office, he scratched BuSpar off his list of drug options.

When I drove Bryce to the doctor after his appendix ruptured, I had the opportunity to ask questions about his anxiety medications. Based on that discussion, I came to the realization that pharmaceutical companies have made a slew of medications available for doctors to prescribe, and the process of finding the right type and brand of medications for an individual's unique biological makeup is a long trial-and-error process. The doctor suggested that Bryce try marijuana to help him wind down and sleep. I was skeptical. It was not many months prior that I had practically thrown Bryce out of my house when I found a marijuana pipe. Not only that, but should Bryce choose to experiment with marijuana, a dispensary staff member with no credentials would be the one to recommend the type and strain of cannabis, as well as the best method of consuming it based on Bryce's self-described condition. Plus, the science is not conclusive. Many researchers still cite evidence that marijuana can cause alterations to brain function, not to mention the fact that marijuana is still illegal under federal law, so employers can fire employees who test positive, even in states like Colorado where the drug is legal. Ultimately, Bryce decided against using marijuana.

Although Bryce is high functioning, the challenges of having any level of anxiety disorder are huge, and recommendations as to how best to treat the condition are varied and confusing. At one extreme are the psychiatrists who insist the condition is biological and can be treated with medication, while at the other extreme are therapists who recommend ridding the body of all medication and then facing and fixing patterns of irrational thought. With one comes the fear of becoming addicted to a drug, of taking a bad drug that ultimately shortens your life, or of changing your brain and becoming someone you are not. On the other hand, there is the reality that by entirely disregarding existing evidence of biological causes and treating only cognitive causes via therapy, and repeating therapy sessions again and again knowing the symptoms may or may not disappear, is in itself debilitating.

Because the causes, diagnoses, and treatments are a mass of contradictions, unknowns, and known unknowns, I was forced to recognize that the answers I was looking for must lie somewhere in the gray area in between.

CHAPTER 4
AWARENESS

The burden of mental disorders continues to grow with significant impacts on health and major social, human rights and economic consequences in all countries of the world.

Over a 12-month period, 27 percent of adults in the US will experience some sort of mental health disorder, making the US the country with the highest prevalence.

Over one's entire lifetime, the average American has a 47.4 percent chance of having any kind of mental health disorder.

— World Health Organization

Anxiety disorders are the most common mental illness in the US, affecting 40 million adults in the United States age 18 and older, or 18% of the population.

— Anxiety and Depression Association of America

was getting my annual eye exam when the optometrist glanced at my chart and noticed I listed *writer* as my profession, so he asked the logical question, "What do you write?" We were moving quickly from the examining room to the lens fitting room, where all I needed to do was pop in some lenses and I would be on my way for another year. So I formulated a concise (albeit vague) response: "I write nonfiction," I said, "and I'm working on a book about the challenges millennials face." The doctor, who appeared to be in his early sixties, stated emphatically that the challenges millennials face are no different from what he, or I, or anyone else throughout history faced at their age. Taken aback by the confidence with which he made this statement, I readily dismissed it, noting that this was one person who would not be buying my book. Yet that quick exchange kept gnawing at me. I could not shake it. I had assumed that it would be as clear to most people that millennials face big, new challenges. I suspect now, however, that like the optometrist, many people do not see that a problem exists, and many, like my husband, say, "What the hell do they have to be stressed about?" It was time to raise my awareness. How widespread is the problem of anxiety in young people?

The slew of data that has accumulated over the past few years is definitive: Teens and twentysomethings are highly stressed and anxious—dangerously so. According to a survey conducted in August 2012 for the American Psychological Association (APA), 39 percent of millennials say their stress has increased in the past year, and 52 percent say stress has kept them awake at night in the past month. More people in the Millennial Generation than any other report being diagnosed with depression or other anxiety-related conditions by their healthcare providers. Millennials also report that they "do not have the support they need to make lifestyle and behavior changes to improve their health and help them cope."[5] And although Generation Z are thought to be more realistic than their predecessors, the millennials, they are already reporting extreme levels of stress during the school year, stress levels that exceed what their parents report.[6]

Living beings are hardwired to respond to stress (recall the fight or flight response), so to a certain extent, stress is a useful tool—a normal reaction to a perceived threat. The hypothalamus (a small region of the brain that controls the autonomic nervous system) sets off an alarm, which, in turn, triggers the adrenal glands to release a surge of hormones, resulting in an accelerated heart rate, elevated blood pressure, and a rise in blood glucose levels. This biological process enhances the brain's ability to use the glucose and increases the availability of tissue repairing substances. Thus, when it becomes necessary to escape the fury of a woolly mammoth or (nowadays) to endure the critical stare of an expectant audience, the process works like a dream. However, when the perceived threat cannot be abated in a reasonable amount of time, there can be negative physical and emotional impacts—trouble sleeping and controlling the emotions; headaches, ulcers, and other digestive disorders; forgetfulness, sexual dysfunction, and irregular menstruation; even heart disease, stroke, and a weakened immune system, which can open the door to other serious illnesses like cancer.

The APA identifies three types of stress, each with its own characteristics and symptoms. Acute stress is the most common type and is easily treated and managed. It stems from the demands and pressures imposed from the recent past as well as demands and pressures anticipated in the near future. In other words, this stress results from having to face the everyday challenges of life, particularly on days when there are multiple challenges of a critical nature in combination with unknowns that follow in close succession. While acute stress can be invigorating, it can also result in symptoms that include emotional distress (anxiety and depression), muscular problems (headache and backache), and stomach issues, as well as elevated blood pressure, dizziness, or shortness of breath. Acute stress can be managed; the

Mayo Clinic recommends several means to do so, including following a healthy diet, getting regular exercise, using relaxation techniques, and having healthy friendships and a sense of humor.

Episodic acute stress is a more severe type of stress that is often manifested in chronic worriers and people with Type A personalities. The emotional symptoms include overarousal, short-temperedness, irritability, and tension on an ongoing basis. Sufferers often consider these characteristics to be ingrained in their personalities, so they resist treatment; however, professional treatment is often the only way to find relief from these emotional symptoms, as well as physical ones—persistent tension headaches, migraines, hypertension, chest pain, and heart disease.

Stress is most dangerous when it falls into the chronic stress category. Chronic stress develops when an individual feels hopelessly trapped in an extremely difficult situation for a long period of time with little to no hope of finding resolution. A person might feel trapped in a dysfunctional family, in poverty, or in an unhappy marriage, for example. Others might be in the emotional aftermath of a severe childhood experience. According to the APA, this chronic stress "kills through suicide, violence, heart attack, stroke and, perhaps, even cancer. People wear down to a final, fatal breakdown."[7] Like many others, I experienced chronic stress when trapped in an unbearable work environment. Fortunately, despite episodes of hopelessness, I was able to escape, but not long afterward I discovered a noninvasive form of cancer in my mammary gland. After a lumpectomy and a year conscientiously avoiding stress, eating a healthy diet, and exercising regularly (as prescribed by my oncologist), I remain cancer free. For those who are not able to escape, however, chronic stress is difficult to treat and typically requires extended medical attention, as well as behavioral treatment and stress management.

While stress is a serious concern in and of itself, it can also lead to an anxiety disorder, which (Bryce discovered) is more life altering and difficult to treat. The APA provides what I have found to be a typical definition of anxiety: "an emotion characterized by feelings of tension, worried thoughts, and physical changes like increased blood pressure." I prefer the more descriptive definition from existential psychologist Rollo May: "Anxiety is a reaction to a threat to the existence of one's self as a human being, or to values that one identifies with that existence." Thus, anxiety is directly related to our very existence and sense of the self. Stated in another way, animals and humans both experience fear, and it is a normal and necessary response to an immediate threat. Fear, says May, "is specific, objective and can be defined." The human experience is different from that of an animal. We have the ability to worry about our fears and anticipate future suffering, so the human fear response can be irrational or disproportionately acute in relation to the perceived threat. This is anxiety. Anxiety, says May, is "vague," "diffuse," and "a condition in which we feel threatened as if the very foundation of existence had been knocked out from under us. The very notion of anxiety implies our powerlessness to meet the threat. In its full-blown form, anxiety is an excruciating painful experience."[8]

In terms of symptoms, the APA says that people with anxiety disorders usually have recurring intrusive thoughts or concerns and may avoid certain situations out of worry. Meg Jay, clinical psychologist and author of *The Defining Decade*, describes people with anxiety as frequently and chronically tense, moody, anxious, and sensitive. Jay, who works regularly with anxiety-laden twentysomethings, finds that they are prone to sadness, worry often, and tend to see everything in a negative light.[9] Over forty million Americans suffer from anxiety disorders, 75 percent first experiencing the illness by age twenty-two. These alarming numbers only represent those who qualify as clinically anxious. Because there is still a stigma associated with the illness, many go untreated, so the number is undoubtedly much higher.

Stress can cause anxiety, and according to Mayo Clinic research, anxiety disorders can trigger depression.[10] Depression is described as an overwhelming sadness that interferes with people's ability to conduct daily life, negatively impacting them and those who care about them. The condition is referred to as major depression when those feelings interrupt the ability to work, sleep, study, eat, and enjoy life. The diagnosis of persistent depressive disorder is ascribed to those who experience symptoms of major depression for at least two years. Depression typically requires medication and psychotherapy, but even when properly treated, depression can lead to suicide, as blatantly evidenced by the recent, highly publicized deaths of celebrities such as Jovan Belker, a player for the Kansas City Chiefs (age twenty-five); fashion designer Alexander McQueen (age forty); and actor/comedian Robin Williams (age sixty-three). According to the American College Health Association (ACHA) the suicide rate among young adults, ages fifteen to twenty-four, has tripled since the 1950s, and suicide is now the second most common cause of death among college students.[11]

One in four young adults between the ages of eighteen and twenty-four have a diagnosable mental illness, and more than one out of four college students have been diagnosed or treated by a professional for a mental health condition within the past year.[12] Of all the mental health issues facing college students today, anxiety disorders and depression are the most common. Statistics from 2012 indicate that 44 percent of college students experienced symptoms of depression that year.[13] In a 2012 ACHA survey, students reported the three factors that most influenced their individual academic performance were stress (29 percent), sleeping difficulties (20.6 percent), and anxiety (20.2 percent), significantly outweighing all other factors.[14] Even more concerning are the findings of a 2013 study by the American College Counseling Association, which state that 95 percent of the counseling center directors at the 203 four-year universities surveyed report "the recent trend toward a greater number of students with severe psychological problems continues to be true on their campuses." Those respondents also reported sixty-nine suicides that year. Some surprising details related to that survey are that 80 percent of the suicide victims had not sought counseling, 71 percent of them were male, and 77 percent were Caucasian.[15] While most of these statistics relate only to students who have been diagnosed as clinically anxious or depressed, according to the ACHA survey, there are many others who report having felt so depressed that it was difficult to function (33.4 percent of women and 26.7 percent of men) and who have felt overwhelming anxiety (56.3 percent of women and 40 percent of men).[16]

The growing mental health issues facing today's youth are exacerbated by the unhealthy ways they often choose to manage those issues. While there is some evidence to indicate that alcohol use is slowly declining, the use of illicit drugs and the nonmedical use of prescription drugs are clearly on the rise. The nonmedical use of prescription drugs (NMPD), particularly amphetamines or stimulants (like Adderall), depressants or sedatives (like Valium), and opioids or pain relievers (like oxycodone), is rampant. Although research identified the trend toward NMPD as early as 2006, the problem has never been fully addressed.[17] According to a 2010 study involving 363 universities "approximately one in three university students have used prescription drugs without a doctor's prescription. Pain medication (22.4%) was the number one misused prescription drug followed by stimulants (17.5%). Almost half of university students reported using NMPDs with alcohol," which increases the side effects, and subsequently, the risk.[18]

Accessibility seems to be the root of the problem. Most young people who take NMPDs access them the same way my son did. Because he was over eighteen years old, he was able to go to a psychiatrist and take a test for attention deficit disorder (ADD). The controversy over whether ADD is overdiagnosed is still raging; I would say, "Yes, it is."

Once he had the paperwork in hand to confirm the results, he could get prescription refills from any doctor in any state at any time. In fact, he took the prescription to one MD in Florida who, out of negligence I presume, gave him three times the prescribed dosage. The irony is that Bryce, who as a child was always attentive and able to complete multistep activities at home with no issue, who as a boy never had disciplinary problems on the athletic field or in the classroom, and who as a teenager could sit calmly for hours studying for advanced classes, was actually diagnosed with ADD. The sad truth is that once Bryce legally became an *adult* at age eighteen, unbeknownst to his parents, he could convince a doctor to prescribe a mind-altering and addictive drug that he could take unsupervised whenever and at whatever dosage he chose, and he could easily trade Valium or any other prescription painkillers, amphetamines, or depressants with his buddies.

Recent studies illustrate how easily young people get access to prescription drugs: 5.3 percent of college students are prescribed attention deficit hyperactivity disorder (ADHD) medications, and 61.7 percent of those students reported diverting (sharing, selling, or trading) their prescription stimulants.[19] According to the most recent survey released by the Substance Abuse and Mental Health Services Administration (SAMHSA), "Fully 55% of people aged 12 and older who had used prescription pain relievers for non-medical reasons in the past year received them from a friend or relative for free."[20]

Interestingly, the SAMHSA survey also indicates that the increase in the use of NMPDs is largely driven by an increased rate of marijuana use. Therefore, it would not be a leap to infer that the rapidly growing legalization and acceptance of marijuana is further impacting the way in which young people view use (or misuse) of prescription drugs. Bryce agrees, explaining that when he takes Adderall and Xanax, he is able to push hard all day, but when the workday is over, he wants to relax—immediately. "And marijuana gives you that." Wary of the consequences, however, Bryce is avoiding this strategy. He knows that, "When people smoke weed continuously, over time they become numb to everything, even their desire and drive to be successful." Thus, for a generation already struggling for direction, the use of marijuana could become what former US Representative Patrick J. Kennedy describes as "a slow train to getting nowhere." By legalizing marijuana, we're setting up a permissive environment, Kennedy explained on *The Colbert Report* (February 14, 2014). Thereby, we do our children an injustice. "With the anxiety level of our young people, the stress of our kids, we're just adding something else that in the short run may make them feel better, but in the long run is really going to cost them and cost our country."[21]

The illegal use of prescription drugs for either recreational purposes or, in Bryce's case, self-medication (that is, to improve study or test-taking capabilities and cope with stress) is considered safe and void of long-term side effects by the majority of millennials and, I venture to say, the rising Z generation as well. These young people typically reason that the drugs are legal because they were originally obtained from a physician. Plus, look around—they are *en vogue*. Young people can purchase drug-related fashion clothing anywhere online, from heavy metal websites to eBay and Amazon. Selections run the gamut from a blue T-shirt with a big, yellow smiley face that reads, "I Took My Xanax," to a simple white T-shirt with the words "Keep Calm and Focus on Amphetamine." I have also seen an emblem that looks like the Krispy Kreme logo, but instead of the company name, it says "Amphetamine," and instead of "donuts," it says, "Go Nuts." If you prefer a jersey, you can get one with a number and the name "Adderall" or "Vicodin" across the back. And then there is the baseball cap that advertises "I ♥ Opioids."

Interestingly, it is now fashionable to wear the label for prescription drugs, but it is still taboo to admit to having a mental illness. According to a 2008 article on college and mental illness, students cited stigma as the most significant barrier to seeking treatment.[22] While there have been some efforts to change the overall perception of mental illness in America—celebrity revelations of mental health issues, for example, and President Barack Obama's proclamation of May 2014 as National Mental Health Awareness Month—the stigma remains. Melissa Thompson agrees. She left a career on Wall Street to start a consumer healthcare technology company designed to make mental healthcare more accessible and affordable through technology. Thompson launched TalkSession, Inc. because she knows that "mental illness-related stigmas are still pervasive and affect not only the afflicted, but family members and friends."[23] While all the long-term effects of taking NMPDs are not yet known, what experts do know is that:

- Use of stimulants over an extended amount of time can increase the risk of cardiovascular problems and strokes, and has been associated with depression, hostility, and paranoia.
- With long-term use, a person can become either physically or psychologically dependent on Adderall.[24]
- Tolerance to depressants can develop rapidly so that larger doses must be taken to achieve the same effect, potentially resulting in coma or death by overdose.[25]
- Opioids are highly addictive. They can create a short-lived feeling of euphoria and drowsiness, which makes the user crave more. Prolonged use can increase the risk for premature death and serious health complications.[26]
- Students who use NMPDs are more likely to commit suicide and have been shown to have greater odds of battling suicidal thoughts throughout their lifetime.[27]

A 2014 *USA Today* article presents compelling evidence that teens are also at risk due to stress, anxiety, and depression. The paper cites a report from the APA that is considered to be the most comprehensive national look at stress in teens to date, which concludes that only 37 percent of teens exercise or walk to manage stress, and 28 percent play sports, while many more choose less healthy activities like playing video games (46 percent) and surfing the Internet (43 percent). The APA CEO and clinical psychologist Norman Anderson fears that by mirroring their parents' stress habits—eating poorly and not getting enough sleep and exercise—teens threaten the future of their generation. The report warns that because of stress and stress management problems, teens are being physically and emotionally impacted, and if we do not take action to reverse the trend, the result will be chronic illness, poor health, and shorter lifespans.

The article goes on to cite a *Child Trends* literature review of mental health among US adolescents released last year, which found that one in four high school students exhibit mild symptoms of depression, including "persistent irritability, anger, withdrawn behavior and deviations from normal appetite or sleep patterns." Furthermore, "29% of high school students in grades 9-12 reported feeling sad or hopeless almost every day for two weeks or more over the past year." For the skeptics among us, having teens self-report their feelings renders the results suspect. However, the article goes on to say that "while one might argue it's very easy to say everything is affected by stress, what's interesting is they're not doing that. . . . They're differentiating between the things they believe are negatively impacted by stress vs. others." For example, "Only 10% believe lower grades are due to stress." In the end, the numbers speak for themselves. One final statistic regarding teen stress is perhaps the most alarming: A study published in a 2012 volume of the *Clinical Psychological Science* journal found that suicide attempt rates are significantly higher in adolescents ages thirteen to seventeen than in emerging adults (ages eighteen to twenty-three) or adults (twenty-four to thirty).[28]

The data clearly demonstrates that anxiety and depression are real, widespread, and on the rise. NMPD use is rampant, and these drugs are widely available and popular. And while some deny it, there are serious consequences. There is a need to raise public awareness, educate the overall population, and offer better treatment resources and tools for stress and anxiety management. And the cause is multifaceted. As Stossel explains, "The truth is that anxiety is at once a function of biology and philosophy, body and mind, instinct and reason, personality and culture."[29]

What I learned, most importantly, is that Bryce and I are not alone. While we may feel isolated because of the stigma associated with mental illness, we clearly are not. We are part of a growing number of people who have been suddenly struck by a mental illness or who are the loved one of someone who has. We are confused by conflicting information. We are reluctant to talk to anyone, as we are wary of repercussions. And we are searching for answers.

CHAPTER 5

REFRAMING MY SEARCH

In our postmodern culture which is TV dominated, image sensitive, and morally vacuous, personality is everything and character is increasingly irrelevant.

— David F. Wells, *No Place for Truth*

At this point in my search, I could describe the nature and extent of the problem, then my thoughts naturally turned to the next question, "Why?" That anxiety and depression have become more problematic within the last decades leads me to believe that the source may be based in historical and societal change. In fact, the more I explore, the more I am convinced that the shift in the way we perceive the world is fundamental to the anxiety problem, because, as theologian and author David F. Wells puts it, "our social context . . . shapes our internal consciousness."[30]

In the last thirty to thirty-five years, the world has seen unprecedented change. As Paul Taylor (age sixty-five), CEO of Pew Research and author of *The Next America* explains:

> *The America of my childhood—with its expanding middle class, secure jobs, intact nuclear families, devout believers, distinct gender roles, polite politics, consensus-building media—is nothing like the country my year-old granddaughter will inherit. Our political, social, and religious institutions are weaker, our middle class smaller, our cultural norms looser, our public debate coarser, our technologies faster, our immigrant-woven tapestry richer, and our racial, ethnic, religious, and gender identities more ambiguous. . . . As a people, we're growing older, more unequal, more diverse, more mixed race, more digitally linked, more tolerant, less married, less fertile, less religious, less mobile, and less confident.*[31]

That there has also been a major shift in philosophical perspective should come as no surprise, as our world has changed so quickly and dramatically as a result of globalization and the technology explosion. "What is outside us shapes what is inside us; what is inside us gives us a framework for understanding the external world that is outside us. In combination these two streams have produced the (post)modern self."[32] And this self, it seems, has become a strange amalgam of optimism, confidence, anxiety, nihilism, and despair. What is this postmodernism? And how has postmodernism shaped internal consciousness?

POSTMODERNISM

Postmodernism can best be understood in relationship to the preceding era, modernism. Modernism is typically associated with the Enlightenment, a sprawling intellectual, philosophical, cultural, and social movement that occurred during the seventeenth and eighteenth centuries across Europe and in America. Over the years that followed the Middle Ages, there was a slow cultural and intellectual shift away from the embodiment of the Church as the sole source of authority toward the view that the universe can be known solely through individual autonomous reason. The Scientific Revolution, which began in 1543 and continued for more than a century, no doubt enabled the Enlightenment, and both movements drew from and informed the humanist system of thought that emphasizes the value of human beings and their ability to solve problems via critical thinking. In the twentieth century, the validity of modern rationalism came into question, however, and by 1960, the mood changed from an embracing rationalistic certainty of the Enlightenment toward a rebellion against all certainty. The mood turned "from Enlightenment arrogance toward postmodern despair."[33]

Modernism is about order and rationality and is concerned primarily with creating order out of disorder; whereas, postmodernism is about fragmentation and instability, and is primarily concerned with deconstruction. One way to comprehend the differences between the two eras is to think about them as American literary critic Frederic Jameson does, in terms of the phases of capitalism and modes of production and technology, which tend to direct certain cultural practices. The first stage, market capitalism (from the eighteenth through nineteenth century), is associated with the steam-driven motor and with realism. The second stage, monopoly capitalism (from the late nineteenth century until the mid-twentieth century), is associated with electric and internal combustion motors, and with modernism. The third stage, multinational or consumer capitalism, emphasizes the marketing, selling, and consuming of commodities and is associated with nuclear and electronic technologies, and with postmodernism.[34]

Another way to expound on what it means to be postmodern is to look at examples from literature, art, film, and theater and see what light the visual arts can shed on our understanding.

Postmodern Literature – Characteristics
Rejects cultural progress and grand narratives—small is good; focuses on the local
Bridges the gap between the literature for high culture (the well-educated elite with the most cultivated taste) and for low culture (the mainstream masses who prefer literature that is more accessible and easily comprehended)
Reacts against literary convention using features such as anachronism, pastiche, fragmentation, vicious circles, and looseness of association like page order
Marked by uncertainty and irony, as well as intellectual and spiritual ambivalence
Addresses subjects such as commercialism, money, power, spiritual aridity, and immoralities
Consciously uses and consequently subverts, in ironic parody, images from history, society, art, and politics

Postmodern Literature – Examples
Kurt Vonnegut, *Breakfast of Champions*
Bret Easton Ellis, *American Psycho*
Thomas Pynchon, *Gravity's Rainbow*
David Foster Wallace, *Infinite Jest*

Postmodern Art – Characteristics
Uses pluralism of style and mixed media
Does not distinguish between art for high culture (the well-educated elite with the most cultivated taste) and for low culture (the mainstream masses who prefer art that is more accessible and easily comprehended)
Allows concept to trump visual presentation

Postmodern Art – Characteristics
Concerned with social justice
Boasts no inherent meaning
Values artists' role over concept and production (anyone can make art)
Uses mundane elements or available found or mass-produced junk
Pieces respond to surroundings / Artists respond to context
Experimental

Postmodern Art – Examples
Andy Warhol's Campbell's Soup Cans
Robert Rauschenberg, *Bed*
Jackson Pollock, *Drip Paintings*
The French National Museum of Contemporary Art, The Specialisation of Sensibility in the Raw Material State into Stabilised Pictorial Sensibility (2009) exhibit, which consists of nine completely empty rooms
Yves Klein, *Blue Monochrome*
John Cage, the silent composition "4'33""

Postmodern Theater – Characteristics
Performs as if productions were real-life events; includes audience participation
Rejects notion of make-believe
Inclusive
Allows outcome to potentially change for each performance
Embraces ideas from culture, society, and history
Relies on mass culture and everyday experience
Can appear as fragments or works in progress

Postmodern Theater and Dance – Examples
David Hare, *Stuff Happens*
Tom Stoppard, *Rosencrantz and Guildenstern Are Dead*
William Forsythe, *The Scott Work* (dance)

Postmodern Film – Characteristics
Combines multiple genres and styles in one film
Parody—imitation of the style of a particular writer, artist, or genre with deliberate exaggeration for comic effect
Flattening of Affect—detachment and lack of emotional reactivity as in the dehumanizing impact of technology
Hyperreality—blurs the lines between what is simulated and what is real
Time Bending—as in rapid intergalactic journeys and time travel
Altered States of Consciousness
Imitation—takes and undermines images from past cinematography
Pastiche—tongue-in-cheek imitation or tribute performed with respect to, or in homage to, other works
Prefabrication—retakes older movie images or sequences
Intertextuality—references other texts to shape the film's meaning

Postmodern Film – Examples
Scary Movie
2001: A Space Odyssey
Monty Python and the Holy Grail
The Matrix Trilogy
Minority Report
Pulp Fiction
Blade Runner
Lucy

The idea that art imitates life is as old as Aristotle, if not older. So much of what we see in the postmodern arts also characterizes what it is like to live in the twenty-first century. The following, for example, are all part of the postmodern experience:

- A disillusionment with life and the power of existing value systems or technologies to effect beneficial change
- A discrediting of authority, expertise, knowledge, and importance of achievement
- A shift in the primary goal of education from the pursuit of knowledge for its own sake to the pursuit of skills for the sake of job acquisition
- The emergence of new technologies, which diminishes the emphasis on quality and craftsmanship
- A desire for novelty, entertainment, even shock and stimulation—instant gratification
- The rejection of grand narratives to explain universal concepts and an embracing of mini-narratives to explain small events and practices: "Postmodern mini-narratives are always situational, provisional, contingent, and temporary, making no claim to universality, truth, reason, or stability."[35]
- The dissolution of the idea that language is transparent, that there is a direct connection between a word and the object the word represents, between the signifier and the signified: In postmodern societies, "The idea of any stable or permanent reality disappears . . ."[36]

The postmodern world highlights the ambivalence of the human experience. The lines are now blurred between what is real and what is not real, what is of good quality and what is of poor quality, what is experimental and what is complete—even what is moral and what is immoral. Postmodernity calls into question the very meaning and purpose of existence, whether life has any meaning or purpose, that is.

THE IMPACT OF POSTMODERNISM

The postmodern world is disconnected. In this technology age, children and adults alike tout the number of friends and followers they have on social media—how connected they are—when, in fact, they are more intrinsically disconnected than ever before: disconnected from work, disconnected from community, and disconnected from family. Industrialization separated people from their work, explains author and theologian David F. Wells. Only under rare circumstances do craftspeople find satisfaction in seeing their work through from beginning to end anymore. And, because we tend to separate the public from the private, our work life from our homelife, we have lost our sense of community too.[37] And no one will argue that the health of the family unit has been ailing for some time now.

Experts are finding that the social networking technologies that promised to restore some connectedness are actually preventing young people from establishing the kind of mature relationships they need, relationships that teach them how to be sensitive and to reciprocate goodwill.[38] Thus we are uprooted and dislodged from those things that once made us connected, those things that gave us a sense of community and a sense of who we are. "What, then, is going to happen to us?" asks Wells. "The simple answer is that we will have to find in ourselves, entirely in ourselves, what we once were given from outside ourselves."[39]

We can attribute much of this disconnectedness and focus on the self to the birth and evolution of the concept of self-esteem. The word self-esteem originated in 1650 and was popularized in the early 1800s by the science of phrenology, the study of brain function. Phrenologists believed that the size and shape of the bumps and indentations of our brains are indicative of a person's mental faculties and character traits, and they assigned self-esteem a bump.[40] In the late nineteenth century, there was a child study movement in which psychologists used the term "self-esteem." Focused on the importance of the self, these psychologists explored the idea of selfhood as essential to a person's freedom and of self-esteem as crucial to one's achievement and success.[41]

Many people trace the beginnings of what is now proving to be an unhealthy level of self-esteem in children to the radical shift in parenting styles that followed the 1946 publication of Dr. Benjamin Spock's *Common Sense Book of Baby and Child Care*. In this book and the editions that follow, Spock promotes a more flexible way of raising children than others promoted in prior decades. "Trust yourself," he tells parents. "You know more than you think you do."[42] Spock was often criticized for encouraging permissiveness, but his advice was largely in reaction to an age of an extremely authoritative and predominantly cold parenting style in which parents were told to operate on a strict schedule and limit the amount of hugging and cradling to ensure their children could function independently. Most of that early advice seems entirely unreasonable to us now. Doctors made recommendations, such as:

Handle the baby as little as possible. Turn it occasionally from side to side, feed it, change it, keep it warm, and let it alone; crying is absolutely essential to the development of good strong lungs. A baby should cry vigorously several times each day.

> — Drs. Lena and William Sadler,
> *The Mother and Her Child* (1916)

At the age of two weeks, the child may be systematically carried about in the arms 2 to 3 times a day, as a means of furnishing additional change in position.

> — Dr. JP Crozer Griffith (1900)

But parents listened because they were afraid. And who can blame them, since 10 to 30 percent of all babies born in 1900 died within a year of birth.[43] Eager for a different approach, Dr. Spock's books left parents craving more, and by the time he died sixty-five years after his first book, it had been translated into forty-two languages with sales close to the fifty million mark. And updated versions of the book continue to sell.[44] Now in its ninth edition, *Dr. Spock's Baby and Child Care* book is a top Amazon seller with a stellar rating.

In 1969, Nathaniel Branden published *The Psychology of Self-Esteem*, a seminal book that was later considered the starting point of the entire self-esteem movement. According to Branden's theory, people should consider self-esteem to be one of the most valuable gifts a human being could receive, and his ideas rapidly took hold, generating tens of thousands of scholarly articles on the subject. Thereby, experts increasingly encouraged parents to build their children's self-esteem in the home by taking a more flexible approach to parenting. Schools, in turn, began providing support by developing programs that would ensure students could achieve success despite their academic talents, which meant building in programs that offer more opportunities for self-expression.[45]

The emphasis on building self-esteem in the home and in the schoolroom continues today, despite the fact that in 2003 researchers found that only a fraction of the articles spawned from Branden's work met rigorous scientific criteria. But by then it was too late. According to Dr. Lauren D. LaPorta, "the damage had been done and these ideas had crept into the mainstream." LaPorta writes:

> *Children were not only praised for less than noteworthy achievements, they were also shielded from any events or experiences that might be damaging to their self-esteem. Healthy competition was replaced by ribbons and prizes just for showing up. Failure was considered*

so potentially harmful to well-being that it had to be avoided at all costs. Doing so, we were promised, would save our children from drug abuse and criminal behavior.[46]

The self-esteem movement continued to strongly influence child development in both theory and practice through the end of the twentieth century, at which time the ideas had been largely debunked. Now, as boomer parents who wholeheartedly adopted these ideas, we are finding out that when played out in real life, they are largely untrue. As a result, our children never learned some of the most important life skills:

- Frustration tolerance
- Hard work
- Persistence
- Self-efficacy—an individual's belief in his or her capacity to execute behaviors necessary to produce specific performance goals

Since our children were never allowed to fail, they do not know how to deal with frustration; and when they do fail, instead of working harder and hanging with it, they tend to give up. And when they are assigned a challenging task, they often do not have the confidence needed to accomplish the task on their own.

Psychologists now reason that boomers grasped on to these new ideas about self-esteem in reaction to what they perceived as having restricted them during their own childhood. So parents and educators alike decided to free their children of those constraints, which meant they would no longer direct children as to their life purpose. Thus, the freedom that the self-esteem movement offered our children also impacted their ability to obtain a sense of who they are. By removing the boundaries, we increase our children's anxiety because we take away what grounds their sense of self.

Like me, maybe you have heard your young adult say, "I don't know who I am." That is because they do not have something to which they can relate and compare themselves, explains psychotherapist and professor of counseling, Elisabeth Nesbit Sbanotto. When we decided to stop interfering in our children's efforts to find their own identity, we removed the best means they have of defining themselves. Parents want their children to be independent spirits, free to explore their sense of self without interference. However, the pendulum swung too far because "psychologically, we need a self to react against, a foundation on which to say, 'I agree,' or 'I disagree.' And when an adolescent has been told their whole lives (relatively speaking) that they can do or be whatever they want to do or be, they have nothing to react against." So their sense of self becomes unstable. What we need to do instead is "reflect back to children who we see and experience them to be and provide them with a foundational sense of self on which they can build."

Another problem is that we do not allow our children to rank themselves, says Sbanotto. Instead, we tell them that everyone is special and everyone is the same. Think about it. As human beings, logic tells us to rank ourselves. So our children naturally look around and compare themselves to others: "I'm smarter than you . . . you're prettier than me . . . you're faster than me . . . I'm skinnier than you." Then they look to authority figures to see if they are right, and we say, "No. Everybody is special." We mean, of course, that everyone has the same value. But that is not what the child is asking. What he or she really wants to know is how they measure up in terms of strengths and weaknesses, abilities and challenges, and so on. And because of our miscommunication, "Their anxiety increases because they don't know if they can't trust themselves or they can't trust their authority figures. They either have to reject authority or doubt their own sense of reality."[47]

So here we are. Our children have been asked to transition into adulthood dependent on their parents' safety net and without a good sense of who they are. This dilemma perpetuates the instability and causes anxiety and depression. As Jay explains in *The Defining Decade*, "There are fifty million twentysomethings in the United States, most of whom are living with a staggering, unprecedented amount of uncertainty . . . and uncertainty makes people anxious."[48] Amidst this uncertainty, the postmodern world ushered in a perception of the self as the center of each individual's universe, which only serves to exacerbate the loneliness and isolation. Psychologist and author Jean Twenge explains:

The growing tendency to put the self first leads to unparalleled freedom, but it also creates enormous pressure to stand alone. This is the downside of the focus on the self—when we are fiercely independent and self-sufficient, our disappointments loom large because we have nothing else to focus on. Generation Me has been taught to expect more out of life at the very time when good jobs and nice houses are increasingly difficult to obtain. All too often, the result is crippling anxiety and crushing depression.[49]

And millennials are finding a myriad of other reasons to feel lonely and isolated. People are: 1) marrying later, divorcing more often, and living longer, 2) setting up more households headed by a single person, and 3) relocating more often, thus severing relationships and/or rendering it difficult to make new friends given time constraints.[50]

Social media only adds steam to the pressure cooker. Users create for themselves the image they want to portray to the world—an image of a life filled with excitement, adventure, and success, limited only by the ability of technology to capture words and display images in a virtual, online world. The self-imposed pressure to keep up with the virtual success of peers is taking its toll. Lucie Green, former editor at

LS:N Global, a services company that provides the latest information on how market and consumer forces are shaping the future, explains, "The constant stream of curated aspirational identities filtered through Instagram is creating a collective anxiety about where we are in life. This is particularly prevalent in millennials, who are not only the heaviest users of social media, but also the most ambitious, with a strong notion of self-entitlement—and with the highest expectations." Neil Dawson, chief strategy officer for a leading UK marketing firm, adds, "The digital age has contributed to our current period of high anxiety by rapidly accelerating change and, undoubtedly, by helping our individual anxieties go viral."[51]

And technology sets up unrealistic expectations, (as if millennials needed more of those). For one thing, the Internet perpetuates the expectation of instant gratification. You want information? You can find it. You want to buy a new product? Just do it. You want to contact someone? Chances are you can reach them instantly via cell phone, text message, online chat, Facebook, Viber, Google+, Skype, or some other channel, as most people are connected 24/7. So ask a millennial to embark on a task that requires an extended period of time to execute, and they are likely to struggle. For another thing, social media sets up an expectation that if you establish an online presence, you can become wildly successful overnight. So the pay-your-dues system of advancement currently at work in corporate America serves only to frustrate young people. They believed us when we told them they are special and that they can be whatever they want to be; plus, they watched Mark Zuckerberg assume billionaire status at age twenty-three. So why should they have to wait?

Finally, millennials are barraged by images of the millionaire lifestyle and have unlimited access to information about people who have more material possessions than they do. The truth is, young people have all of these pent-up unrealistic expectations; at the same time, they are unprepared for real-life relationships and the real-life workplace. The paradox breeds anxiety, anxiety, and more isolation, loneliness, and anxiety.

While the self is becoming increasingly isolated, the self is simultaneously ascending to new levels of significance. Our children now seek knowledge, understanding, morality, even God and the Truth from within themselves. Here is one case in point: A 2011 survey of emerging adults ages eighteen through twenty-three revealed that young Americans no longer feel they are subject to an ultimate morality—60 percent claimed that moral rights and wrongs are a matter of individual opinion.[52] Similarly, people are rejecting formal religion in favor of creating their own spirituality. As recent Pew Research polls show, one-third of millennials self-identify as religiously unaffiliated, the highest percentage of unchurched ever recorded in the US. Of these so-called "nones," roughly a quarter describe themselves as atheists or agnostics; the remainder believe in a supreme being but have no religious affiliation.

"The US is still the most religiously observant nation among the world's great powers. But led by today's young, it's growing more pluralistic and less connected to traditional religious institutions."[53] The Church's efforts to reach millennials (often interpreted as insincere and superficial) have largely fallen flat. Even young Christians are dropping out of church—nearly three out of every five young Christians (59 percent) disconnect from church life, either permanently or for a long period of time after the age of fifteen, according to a Barna Group five-year research study released in 2011 and revealed in David Kinnaman's book *You Lost Me*.[54] Disillusioned, many young people are choosing to construct their own spirituality; however, they are open to a new forum for exploring their beliefs. As Rachel Held Evans, author and millennial advocate stated in a 2013 interview with CNN, "Millennials with a Christian background who have dropped out of church say they are not looking for a hipper version of Christianity, . . . I think what young people are really looking for is not a church that answers all their questions, but a community or place where they feel safe wrestling with these tough questions . . ."[55]

I shared my original book proposal with my dear millennial friend Jen to get her feedback early in the creative process. Before responding, she wanted to better articulate her ideas about how millennials are influenced by the postmodern world, so she phoned a friend. Instead of helping her formulate a response, however, the conversation served only to reinforce the fact that most young people do not see any other way of perceiving the world apart from the self. Feeling discouraged and sad, Jen emailed me back on January 2, 2015: "We are so ingrained in this postmodern world that it's especially difficult to help others recognize it. . . . We as a generation try to understand everything as it relates to us. It is pervasive and becomes so detrimental—especially as we deal with our own crises and refuse to really reflect on God's work through history to help put our problems in perspective."

Through my research, I have become infinitely more aware of what it means to live in the twenty-first century and what it means for our social context to shape our internal consciousness. And I am beginning to wonder if Bryce is emblematic of the growing risk young people face of developing a mental illness in the conditions that are present and increasingly prominent in the postmodern world. Is there a correlation between the ethos becoming more ingrained in our culture and the rising levels of mental illness?

Bryce is like many young people—good looking, intelligent, creative, and proficient with technology. And like many children of Type A parents, he is genetically hardwired to be a perfectionist. He grew up with some boundaries. We established rules about homework and cleaning his room, for example, and we taught him the difference between right and wrong. We expected him to be polite and respectful of others. But we also gave him a great deal of space to decide what to do with his spare time (we did not insist that he find a job, for example), and he had total freedom to decide where to go to college and what degree to pursue. (It was always understood that our children would go to college.) We communicated our high expectations of him, but we also succumbed to the "every kid is a trophy kid" cultural norm, and we have always been his safety net. Bryce is my Eeyore, as he is frequently tense, moody, sad, and negative; sometimes he is entitled; he can be confident but is often unsure; and he is always living in eager anticipation of reaching his goal to be CEO before thirty. He has a big heart, and I am thrilled when he lets that show.

Now place someone with similar characteristics into the postmodern environment. There he feels isolated. He is confronted by overblown images of success and fame 24/7; he feels the constant pressure to compete; and he is frequently frustrated by unrealistic expectations. As a perfectionist, he has some OCD tendencies, but with the help of his family, particularly his big brother, he is managing well. Then he develops some teenage acne, which, try as he might, he cannot control. Then a pretty girl he admires blatantly spurns him for it. Slowly he becomes obsessed by the desire to become the perfect image of his best self. As a result, he develops recurring, intrusive thoughts about his imperfections, and even though he is incredibly self-aware, he does not recognize those thoughts as being self-generated and unreasonable. After college and some therapy, he begins to recognize that his thoughts about what are now occasional and normal skin imperfections are irrational, so he is managing that anxiety. But anxiety still shows up in other places in reaction to adult-life pressures.

So sometimes the anxiety disorder shows up when individuals (even those as self-aware as Bryce) do not see when they are being irrational or when they see they are being irrational but cannot do anything to change the behavior. Bryce has always been self-aware—aware of his spirituality, his emotions, and his body. As a middle-schooler, for example, he did not feel well one day, so I took him to the doctor. During the examination, he explained the symptoms to the doctor and proceeded to expound on the pros and cons of all the medications available on the market to treat them. Based on his research, Bryce deduced which prescription he preferred and pitched his proposal. To my surprise and amusement, the doctor agreed to the recommendation and told Bryce that he should grow up to be a lawyer. Despite his self-awareness, however, years later he could not see how irrational it was to stay in bed paralyzed by anxiety over going out in public with a blemish on his face. It took a psychiatrist to point it out to him; then he was able to process the reality of the situation and learn how to manage his irrational thoughts and subsequent behaviors. This is not easy.

Lane, a millennial friend who does my nails, can attest to that. She describes herself as extremely self-aware. In a recent discussion, she explained that when she has an anxiety attack, she knows that her thoughts and behaviors are irrational, but she cannot control them. "Just the other day, I was shopping at Target," she told me. "I was on my way to the checkout counter when I realized I couldn't go through with it. I walked around Target for three hours before I could check out and go home. I knew that didn't make sense, but there is nothing I could do about it." These stories and others like them taught me that recovery from a mental disorder is a process that takes time, effort, and patience.

Because I am writing this book, I have a good reason to interject the subject of anxiety and depression in conversations with people I meet everyday, and practically everyone I talk to either suffers from similar mental challenges or knows someone who suffers. It seems to me that the uniquely twenty-first century environmental conditions are conducive to anxiety and depression, and thereby either cause, trigger, or exacerbate the problem.

A CALL TO ACTION

As I struggle in my search for answers, I gain insight and draw strength from one of the premier writers, philosophers, and theologians of modern times, G.K. Chesterton. In his *Ballad of the White Horse*, I find encouragement to continue my quest. The ballad is a mystical, epic tale of King Alfred the Great who rallies troops to defeat the pagan Guthrum the Dane and his Viking army. Chesterton repeats the refrain "the sky grows darker yet/And the sea rises higher" several times to remind the reader that although the king knows victory may not be his, he is content to fight for what he believes is right. And even if he is victorious, the sky may still grow dark and the sea may rise yet again.

Building on that theme, Chesterton introduces the image of the White Horse, a statue that represents the moral traditions set in place before time to preserve mankind. King Alfred wins the battle and preserves the White Horse, but later, in his retirement years, he notices that grass and weeds have overtaken the statue again:

> And it fell in the days of Alfred,
> In the days of his repose,
> He bade them keep the White Horse white
> As the first plume of the snows.

> And right to the red torchlight,
> From the trouble of morning grey,
> They stripped the White Horse of the grass
> As they strip it to this day.

Despite King Alfred's efforts, however, before long weeds and fungus overcome the statue again:

And all the white on White Horse Hill
The horse lay long and wan.
The turf crawled and the fungus crept,
And the little sorrel, while all men slept,
Unwrought the work of man.[56]

These words Chesterton wrote in 1911 are pregnant with meaning today. If we fail to clear the growth away from the White Horse now, if we do not set up guideposts to mental and spiritual health in the twenty-first century, all may be lost. The relativism that pervades this era, the connectedness that has slipped away in the context of the postmodern world, may never be regained, as those with knowledge and life experience of what it was like to live prior to the Information Age pass away.

It is the premise of *Escape from Dark Places* that it is our duty and privilege as parents, grandparents, church leaders, and mentors of the rising generations to once again clear the outline of the White Horse. The moral compass has been lost (or misplaced), and despite our good intentions, I suspect in many ways we boomers and even Xers are at fault. On the other hand, we are in a unique position to set the course aright, or at least to initiate the process because:

- Millennials are returning home in droves, yet "our generations aren't at each other's throats. They're living more interdependently than at any time in recent memory, because that turns out to be a good coping strategy in hard times."[57]
- "Millennials seem much more disposed toward cooperation than conflict."[58]
- Millennials are more than anything else "America's most stubborn optimists."[59]

At the same time, it is your responsibility, millennials, to look toward the past to enlighten the present and prepare for the future—to recognize the plight of the postmodern world and willingly adjust for your sake and for the sake of your children.

Change requires a resolve across generations to address the issue of disconnectedness and all that disconnectedness implies. In cooperation, the generations can raise awareness of postmodern challenges, reduce the impact of stress, anxiety, and depression, and help stop the stigma surrounding mental illness.

PART 2
MY SEARCH

CHAPTER 6
GENERATIONAL RESEARCH

Being young has not always carried such a high risk of being anxious, depressed, suicidal, or medicated. Only 1% to 2% of Americans born before 1915 experienced a major depressive episode during their lifetimes, even though they lived through the Great Depression and two world wars. Today, the lifetime rate of major depression is ten times higher—between 15% and 20%. Some studies put the figure closer to 50%.

— Jean M. Twenge, *Generation Me*

B ased on my determination that the rise in anxiety and depression are rooted in historical and social change, my best next step was to conduct a review of generational research and assess the findings in light of my search for answers. The research began with William Strauss and Neil Howe, who are considered pioneers in the field of generational theory. The two men teamed up in 1991 to publish a compilation of biographical sketches, which is the basis for what has evolved into a theory widely known as the Strauss-Howe generational theory. When these two ex-Capitol Hill aides, innately curious about the impact of generations, delved into a five-decade study of American history, they discovered a pattern. The complex, cyclical pattern (or a "convoluted" pattern according to the Publishers Weekly editorial review at the time) is thought to be unique to the history of Anglo-Americans. The pattern consists of eras (or turnings), which recur every two decades or thereabouts. The turnings present themselves in cycles comprised of a "High," and then an "Awakening," followed by an "Unraveling," and finally a "Crisis." The Era of Good Feelings is an example of a high turning (1794-1822); which was followed by the Transcendental Awakening, an awakening turning (1822-1844); and then the Mexican War and Sectionalism, an unraveling turning (1844-1860); and culminating with the Civil War which would clearly be a crisis turning (1860-1865).[60]

Strauss and Howe went on to apply this theory throughout their careers, using it to further analyze cohort differences and predict future impacts. In their second book, which focuses on Gen X, they begin to explore from a historical context what it means to be a particular birth cohort. Later, in their book *The Fourth Turning*, they make the leap from informing to prophesying as they prepare readers for the imminent era of secular upheaval, the Crisis Turning known as the new millennium. Many people are drawn to the sensational nature of the predictions, yet scholars fear the element of prophecy takes the theory too far too soon. I agree, yet the basic tenets of the theory should not be discounted: "Generations that experience similar early-life experiences often develop similar collective personas, and follow similar life-trajectories."[61] Knowing what shapes people is paramount to understanding what makes them tick.

In contrast to Strauss and Howe, Dr. Jean Twenge uses empirical research to strengthen the case for generational theory. Twenge conducted fourteen studies of generational differences in personalities involving 1.2 million people (2006). Based on those studies, she predicts in *Generation Me* that two cohorts, Generation Y and Z in aggregate, will have a difficult time growing up. With the advantage of more time and data—an additional nineteen studies involving a total of eleven million people—Twenge confirms and reinforces her claims (2014).[62] In addition to the sheer volume of data she collected, Twenge is recognized for her unique research methods. Twenge introduced and popularized a method of research whereby researchers track standardized psychological test scores over time. This method, which she termed "cross-temporal meta-analysis," is valuable to generational studies because it enables researchers to compare people of the same age at different points in time, thereby eliminating the need to rely on their recollection of events long past and memories of themselves colored by time. Twenge uses personality scores that date back to the 1960s to measure such personality traits as narcissism and self-esteem. In her second edition of *Generation Me*, Twenge adds supplemental quantitative, as well as more qualitative data.

Twenge's research results are startling. She finds that the bent toward individualism has triggered a standard deviation shift in practically all personality traits toward unhealthy levels of self-esteem and self-focus, as well as anxiety and depression, and a diminished ability to identify with others' emotions and experiences, or empathize. Twenge states definitively that, "When you are born has more influence over your personality than the family you grew up with."[63] The following quote indicates how Twenge's generational theory relates specifically to my research: "Generation Me has the highest self-esteem of any generation, but also the most depression. They are more free and equal, but also more cynical. They expect to follow their dreams, but are anxious about making that happen."[64]

Twenge continues to focus her career on discovering and predicting generational trends because the findings have proven to be of significant intellectual, cultural, and economic interest.[65] While Twenge is clear that the goal should always be to understand people, not to change them, she does recommend change that could ultimately lead to a positive cultural shift. Changes in education and the media, for example, could help reverse the unhealthy trends incited by the individualistic cultural system of the postmodern world, a system that "seems to have crossed the line from individualism to hyperindividualism."[66] Twenge calls specifically for an end to the self-esteem movement, better career counseling, and more support for working parents.[67] Particularly relevant to the study of anxiety and depression is her current research on how increasing use of social media impacts our ability to connect to community.

One of Twenge's contemporaries, Jeffrey Jensen Arnett, is a developmental psychologist and research professor. It is Arnett who identified "emerging adulthood" as a new life phase and subsequently coined the term. This phase is a distinct period of life between adolescence and adulthood when individuals (ages eighteen to twenty-nine) spend an extended period of time exploring life directions. (Note that this life phase only applies in industrialized countries where opportunities for self-exploration can exist.)[68] This theory of development, first published in *American Psychologist* in 2000, has since proven to be seminal, particularly in the potential it provides for better understanding the Millennial Generation and the rising Generation Z birth cohorts. While the rite of passage has long existed, Arnett argues that sweeping demographic shifts of the last half a century have extended this time of exploration. The psychological community grabbed on to Arnett's theory with a vengeance; as a result, Arnett founded the Society for the Study of Emerging Adulthood, a nonprofit solely devoted to understanding human development during these formative years. This extended transition into adulthood clearly delays key life events, including launching from the family home, marrying, having children, seeking a post-secondary education, and finding gainful employment. The growing body of knowledge related to the transition to adulthood will offer a better understanding of what young people are experiencing and why.

Arnett takes a cultural approach to his research; thus, he leans heavily on qualitative methods, preferring interviews to questionnaires because "there is simply no substitute for sitting face-to-face with someone and talking to them about what they have experienced and what it means to them."[69] Early in his career, Arnett developed a curiosity about how young adults perceive of and engage in the world around them. His research began when he and his graduate students interviewed 300 young people in cities across the country, asking questions about what they want to get out of life. In recent research, Arnett adds survey data as well as an international perspective.

The Millennial Generation will soon surpass boomers as the largest living generation in history, so the demand for information has never been greater. And there is no sign that research and marketing firms will disappoint. Barna Group, for example, started the Barna Millennial Project approximately ten years ago and has interviewed over 27,000 millennials in 206 studies.[70] The firm, which primarily serves churches and nonprofits, provides subscribers with research, training, and resources. Two popular and recent books are *Churchless,* which provides strategies the churched can use to reach the growing number of unchurched in today's culture, and *You Lost Me*, which outlines negative perceptions of the church and explains why young Christians feel forced to leave.

The Pew Research Center is another organization that has contributed heavily to the discussion of generational impacts on culture.

As a nonprofit think tank, Pew Research uses a variety of techniques to gather volumes of data, including public opinion polling and media content analysis in order to "generate a foundation of facts that enriches the public dialogue and supports sound decision-making."[71] Articles like "Millennials in Adulthood" use data to describe general social trends that differentiate generations, while other articles address diverse topics more specifically, from education and politics to the workplace and public policy.

Pew Research executive vice president Paul Taylor demonstrates how generational studies are being used to inform public policy in his book *The Next America: Boomers, Millennials, and the Looming Generational Showdown*. Taylor translates a glut of data in an effort to "illuminate the demographic, economic, social, cultural, and technological changes that are remaking not just our politics but our families, livelihoods, relationships, and identities."[72] The book focuses on the two largest generations, as they stand at odds with each other over a myriad of competing interests—the rise in human longevity, the fall of human birthrates, the condition of Medicare and Social Security, political gridlock, income inequality, and the list goes on. The central question Taylor explores is how our country can "honor our commitments to the old without bankrupting the young and starving the future." Despite the book title, Taylor contends that neither side has the stomach for a showdown. The best thing we can do, he says, is "frame the challenge in generational terms," as parents and children having an "equity argument," and then, with strong presidential leadership, odds are we can reach consensus.[73]

Though young, the field of generational studies is proving to be legitimate. Data abounds, and though not yet time-tested, the discipline is rich with possibilities. Knowing what makes another generation tick has proven benefits. For example, the information is used to:

- Market products and services to a particular target audience
- Direct research and development efforts in anticipation of future need, in terms of medicine and technology, for example
- Determine how pedagogy adjusts in theory and practice to meet the changing needs of young minds
- Enable successful talent management and succession planning in the workplace
- Ensure generations have a voice through party platforms and the election process
- Inform public policy

At last I had found a path to discovery that spoke directly to my search. Generational theory legitimately serves to illuminate our understanding of anxiety and depression in light of historical and cultural change and opens the door to understanding what makes the generations tick.

CHAPTER 7
THE SOCIETAL DISCONNECT

Our Generation has had no Great war, no Great Depression. Our war is spiritual. Our depression is our lives.

— Chuck Palahniuk, *Fight Club*

GENERATIONAL THEORY

Generational theory can tell us how history and culture have changed us and can provide a means of repairing some societal disconnects. Generally, the value of this social science lies in its ability to categorize birth cohorts by identifying events, trends, and other cultural phenomena that shaped them and then to describe the behaviors that characterize each group. It is a means of understanding other generations in relation to our own.

As a thirtysomething graduate school teaching assistant and mother of three, I learned just how critical it is that we have intergenerational understanding. One day when I was standing in front of a Composition 1 class introducing Kurt Vonnegut's book *Cat's Cradle*, I raised the question, "Why does Vonnegut start his novel by having the narrator say, 'Call me Jonah. My parents did, or nearly did. They called me John.'" Well, the answer that resonated from the back of the room was, "Who cares?" I could not fathom this. Vonnegut's allusion to the prophet Jonah in the Bible and his reference to the first line of *Moby Dick*, "Call me Ishmael," cuts to the core of the main theme of the entire novel. I recovered and moved on but eagerly shared the story with my teaching professor later that day: "I can't understand these kids," I said. "Why do they come to college if they aren't interested in learning anyway?" My professor simply said, "You *have* to understand them." I knew she was right.

I often see comments on blogs and online articles about generations in which readers complain that by generalizing, we water down information and render it meaningless. Granted, by categorizing, we generalize, but categorization is what provides us with a means of talking about and making sense of groups of things or people that have commonalities. We generalize when we talk about characteristics shared by a particular gender, ethnic group, or clique, for example. While generational categorizations may seem arbitrary, they are, in fact, based on observable behaviors and are important for understanding people groups. As one generational consulting services organization puts it, "Because members of a generation are shaped in lasting ways by the eras they encounter as children and young adults, they also tend to share some *common beliefs and behaviors,* including basic attitudes about risk taking, culture and values, civic engagement, and family life."[74]

Author and speaker Chuck Underwood explains the value of generational studies this way: He says that our core values are established during our formative years and remain largely unchanged. Underwood's key point is that these values continue to influence decisions, lifestyle preferences, and even career choices throughout our lives.[75] In the field of psychology, "formative years" refers to the years from birth through age eighteen. Though for millennials, as we saw with the theory of emerging adulthood, the formative years may extend to age twenty-nine. Given the inexact science of generational studies, the years assigned to each group vary slightly based on the source, but the insights and conclusions are the same. That said, be aware that while I talk about boomers, Generation Xers, millennials, and the up-and-coming Generation Z, any discussion about your generation may not fully describe you; however, I expect you will see glimpses of yourself and people you know in each cohort and will get a sense of where you fall in the sliding scale from "share all the characteristics of my generation" to "share very few of the characteristics of my generation."

The G.I. Generation

Birth Years	1901-1924
Formative Years	1901-1942
Age in 2016	92-115
Core Values / Characteristics	Loyalty, Hard Work, Patriotism, Respect for Authority, Self-Reliance, Civic Obligation

The Name

Based on Army inventory lists drafted in the early twentieth century, the name "G.I." originated with the United States Army's logistics department, which used the term to denote military items that were made from galvanized iron. During WWI, the term "G.I. can" referred to German artillery shells and bombs, and "G.I." to military general issue items such as soap, shoes, and brushes. The meaning continued to evolve and expand during WWII until it became so generalized that people used it to describe practically anything related to an American soldier. Eventually anyone serving in the Army or Air Force was called a "G.I. Joe."

Some people considered it demeaning to call a soldier a G.I. Take General Douglas MacArthur, for example. When the general's surgeon called MacArthur's troops "G.I.s," he responded, "Don't ever do that in my presence. . . . G.I. means 'general issue.' Call them soldiers." Others argued the term was derogatory because it was also used to describe men who were crude or uncouth.[76] Nonetheless, Dwight D. Eisenhower's speech delivered on May 8, 1945, from the Allied headquarters in Reims, France, popularized the term:

> *Merely to name my own present and former principal subordinates in this theater is to present a picture of the utmost in loyalty, skill, selflessness and efficiency. . . . But all these agree with me in the selection of a truly heroic man of this war. He is GI Joe and his counterpart in the air, the navy and the merchant marine of every one of the United Nations.*[77]

In that same year, United Artists released *The Story of G.I. Joe*, starring Burgess Meredith and Robert Mitchum, a movie that received four Academy Awards and established Mitchum as one of the world's foremost actors. The movie, in turn, inspired Hasbro's G.I. Joe action figures some twenty years later, forever ingraining "G.I." into the American psyche. It wasn't until 1998 that a book by Tom Brokaw, a renowned American journalist and former anchor of *NBC Nightly News*, displaced "G.I. Generation" with a more positive identifier that emphasizes their heroism: "The Greatest Generation."

The Historical and Social Context

The turn of the century marked the end of the frontier. The West was won, the Indians had surrendered, and the buffalo were gone. American farmers were growing more food than any farmers in the world, and the US had become the number one manufacturer of steel. Henry Ford had produced the first gasoline engine car and established the Ford Motor Company, while the railroad system spanning North America continued to grow. As the century progressed, more people started communicating via the telephone and lighting their homes and places of business with electricity.[78] In 1914, the assassination of Archduke Franz Ferdinand triggered a series of events that ignited the First World War (1914-1918). The US declared war in 1917, leading the allies to victory. Afterwards, Americans breathed a sigh of relief as the country entered into an exciting new decade—the Roaring Twenties.

For the first time, people could buy on credit, and there were plenty of products to buy. The economic advantages of American manufacturing coupled with Henry Ford's timesaving assembly line techniques enabled mass production of gasoline-powered automobiles and made it possible for the average citizen to afford one. Women eagerly purchased modern conveniences, such as electric machines for washing and drying clothes, while more and more families bought radios so they could gather around and listen to the latest news and music in the evening. And for a little entertainment outside of the home, Hollywood introduced the moving picture show.

Less than 1 percent of Americans owned stock, so the rich grew exceedingly richer. The urban working class and middle class saw some financial gains as well, but American farmers struggled throughout the decade as post-war overproduction resulted in surplus crops and falling prices. Increased spending led businesses and manufacturing industries to keep expanding until stock prices far exceeded realistic values. Further to the detriment of the economy, an average of 600 banks failed every year between 1921 and 1929. "By 1929 farming families—roughly a quarter of the US population—were desperately struggling." And of the 27.5 million families in the US, 78 percent (21.5 million) could only afford the bare necessities.[79] Wall Street crashed on October 29, 1929; investors pulled out, and by 1930 half of all banks closed their doors. The country spiraled into depression, leaving thirteen to fifteen million Americans unemployed.

Americans were bewildered and confused, and while there was panic and fear, there was none of the violence and looting we see today. "Americans believed that they were somehow responsible for their situation and that they had to endure it without resorting to such extremes."[80] Wanda Bridgeforth, who lived with her family in Chicago in the '30s, describes her unemployed father as broken and humiliated. Even with a degree in chemistry, he could not get a job. To support the family, Wanda's mother found work as a live-in domestic but had to send her grade-school-age daughter away. Sometimes Wanda lived with family and sometimes with strangers. She remembers her mother telling her, "This is the way it has to be. So we either do it and survive or don't do it and don't survive."[81]

Studs Terkel, the author of an oral history of the 1930s, remembers the onset of the Great Depression as a gradual wearing away at people's livelihood and self-worth. Studs's mother owned a fifty-room hotel known as the Wells-Grand, which was generally filled to capacity. In the '30s, she watched the roster dwindle and guests' spirits fail as they spent more and more time in the lobby playing cards and checkers, tempers on edge. "The suddenly-idle hands blamed themselves, rather than society. True, there were hunger marches and protestations to City Hall and Washington, but the millions experienced a private kind of shame when the pink slip came. No matter that others suffered the same fate, the inner voice whispered, 'I'm a failure.'"[82] And as author and historian Christopher Lasch says, "Hardly any of the observers of the Thirties sensed a revolutionary mood among the people. Almost all describe the same sense of dismay and disorientation, futility and shame. Being unemployed seems to have been experienced more often as a humiliation than as evidence of class exploitation. A matter of personal fault."[83]

Leaders in Washington were bewildered too. President Herbert C. Hoover was elected in 1928 on a platform that included a mandate to shrink the government back to prewar size and stop public interference with private business. He held that the American system was based on "rugged individualism" and "self-reliance," and that Washington's attempts to resolve poverty and unemployment would only undermine people's character by making them dependent on the government. And while many of the reforms that would be executed under the next administration may have already been structured under Hoover's direction, he either lacked the resolve or the power to act. But when President Franklin D. Roosevelt assumed office in 1933, he immediately took action, declaring "the only thing we have to fear is fear itself."

The day after his inauguration, Roosevelt imposed a bank holiday that suspended all banking transactions. Four days later, member banks in Federal Reserve cities reopened. Banks that controlled 90 percent of the country's banking resources had resumed operations, and citizens were depositing money again. This was probably the turning point of the Depression, said political economist Raymond Moley. "When people were able to survive the shock of having all the banks closed, and then see the banks open up, with their money protected, there began to be confidence. . . . Most of the legislation that came after didn't really help the public. The public helped itself, after it got confidence."[84]

The measures Roosevelt enacted within his first one hundred days in office, which came to be known as the New Deal, represented a radical shift to centralized government. It was the first of many legislative experiments. Some succeeded and many failed, and ultimately none of them pulled America out of the economic downfall. But the fact that Roosevelt was making an effort made a difference. And the thirty speeches broadcast over the radio, Roosevelt's fireside chats, inspired hope and confidence overall. On December 7, 1941, the Japanese bombed Pearl Harbor and the US entered WWII. The war stimulated American industry and ended the Great Depression.

Connecting with the G.I. Generation

It is difficult for my children to get a real sense of what the G.I. Generation was like. They had a few brief visits with their great-grandparents when they were quite young, but since work prevented us from living close to family, there was not enough exposure to instill an appreciation of the personality traits that made the generation great. Our children can certainly read books and watch period films, and we should encourage them to do so. But what we really need to do is tell them stories.

I was fortunate to have been able to spend quality time with all four of my grandparents and to meet all my husband's grandparents as well. Some of my earliest memories are of watching my Grandmother Slaughter (Stella) make quilts. As a baby, I stacked empty wooden spools of thread while she cut remnants from material she used to make doll clothes and stuffed animals for us, and when I was old enough to handle a needle, she taught me to embroider—or she tried. I was never very good at it, but that was not what mattered. The family captured this story and many others like it in a book we wrote about Stella and presented it to her on her eightieth birthday. It turns out that the book was not only something she enjoyed reading over and over again, but it also provided intergenerational talking points and preserved memories in a format that will be easy to share across generations over time.

By sharing stories in a generational context, somehow what the young people typically disregard as old-fashioned suddenly takes on new meaning. Stories of how Stella grew up on a farm as the youngest of eight, for example, and of how she raised four children in the midst of war and depression give substance to the values we see on a generational core values chart—hard work and self-reliance. What does that look like exactly? For the Thompson family, that meant working in the industry hardest hit by the Depression—farming. The Thompsons raised all the food the family needed to survive. Parents and children worked side by side plowing the fields, killing and dressing hogs, making syrup, raising livestock, cooking, and sewing. And they spent fun times together too, attending church fellowships, singing, and dancing; and they all played instruments.

Although the kids had some freedom to choose their chores (inside or out, for example), everyone had to work in the field at harvest time. Even at age five, little Stella helped pick cotton. Papa "got 'em all fed and raised," Stella remembered. "Always had plenty to eat and clothes. Had what everybody else around us had." I understood what "plenty" meant when Stella told me the story of the time she got to accompany her papa on the twelve-mile wagon ride to town to sell their surplus vegetables. Once they got to town, Papa bought Stella a Coke. When they got home and Mama found out, she was appalled and scolded Papa because it was not her turn to have a Coke. It was her sister Maggie's turn.

Stella and Neill were married on November 23, 1930, in the heart of the Depression. Neill built levies and found various other jobs to survive, typically through Roosevelt's New Deal programs. As a result, the family frequently had to pick up and move away from their home to take advantage of temporary work opportunities, which made raising four children a challenge. Many times the family was forced to endure the squalid living conditions of the tent cities, but they traveled together nonetheless, determined to keep the family unit intact. Between jobs, their loyalty to family always brought them back home, and eventually they both found sustainable work that enabled them to stay home permanently. In 1968, Neill and Stella were able to build and own the brick home where they lived out the rest of their lives.

On the other side of the family were my Bigmama and Papa Hamaker (Ivy and Claude). I spent many a day on their front porch shelling purple hull peas and pecans, looking forward to homemade biscuits for breakfast, and with any luck, chicken and dumplings for dinner. Even as a child, experiencing those lazy days of busy work and quiet conversation enabled me to fashion a generation of frugal, hardworking men and women committed to community, devoted to country, and loyal to them both. However, there were some values I struggled to comprehend, as they contrasted so sharply with my own; for example, I repeatedly petitioned Claude to buy Ivy a new stove, my argument being that it would "make her life a little easier." He never relented, and only looking back now do I begin to understand why.

While I was one of the youngest grandchildren in my family, my husband was one of the oldest in his. This birth order enabled him to spend time with his grandparents during their more active years. There was many a summer day he spent working by his Grandpa Millard Watkins's side tending the cattle and chickens. Millard worked four chicken houses, raising 33,000 pullets, seven times a year—manually. What that means is that seven times a year he scraped up 48,000 square feet of chicken litter and replaced it with clean shavings. Between batches he built the cardboard feeding boxes that extended the length of each house. After the baby chicks arrived, each day was scheduled around feeding times when he pushed the wheelbarrow down the center aisle of each house, stopping regularly to bend down and scoop feed and to kill or dispose of sick and dead chickens. As busy as those times were, any downtime was spent with family. For my husband, that meant peaceful times with his grandpa fishing at the pond.

For as long as anyone can remember, the extended family had Sunday dinner at Grandma Delma Watkins's house. There was always a spread. The adults claimed their seats at the big table. The youngest kids sat around the small table and kitchen counter, but graduated to the big table as they grew up. Delma encouraged everyone to take all the food they wanted but insisted that they eat all the food they took. She made sure nothing went to waste. The conversation, which revolved around politics and the Watkins's view of world events, moved from the kitchen to the front porch after dessert. I recall being introduced to Sunday dinner when my husband and I first started dating. Although I did not always agree with the Watkins's, I found the tradition charming. It reminded me of the gatherings at Stella's house. There were chicken legs, chicken livers, and other fixin's spread across the big kitchen table, and after dinner the adults played rook and dominoes. The house was abuzz with conversation, while Neill's favorite Herb Alpert album played on the record player in the background.

What my husband and I marvel about most when we talk about our grandparents' generation is their stoicism. Despite the World Wars, the Great Depression, and all the hard work that was required of them, they never complained; complaining was simply not part of the culture. Instead of talking about themselves when we were together, our grandparents spent time focusing on us, getting to know us as individuals. They made each of their grandchildren feel special, not just because we were their grandchildren but also because they had invested themselves in us and could praise each of us for our strengths and unique qualities.

The Silent Generation

Birth Years	1925-1945
Formative Years	1925-1963
Age in 2016	71-91
Core Values / Characteristics	Conformity, Teamwork, Loyalty, Patriotism, Peace, Financial Stability, Quality, Willingness to Sacrifice for Common Good

The Name

The name "Silent Generation" first appeared in the cover story of the November 1951 edition of *Time* magazine and took root when, in 1973, historian William Manchester wrote, "Never had American youth been so withdrawn, cautious, unimaginative, indifferent, unadventurous— and silent."[85] Then, when Strauss and Howe used the name in their 1992 book, *Generations: The History of America's Future, 1584 to 2069*, it stuck.

The Historical and Social Context

The oldest silents spent many of their formative years in the throes of the Great Depression, as families struggled to pull themselves up by their bootstraps. Even though New Deal policies provided some economic relief, the Depression dragged on. The unemployment rate still hovered around 15 percent in 1939. And many of those who saw their fathers go off to war were now off to war themselves, a war that claimed over 670,000 lives.

During WWII, more women than ever before entered the workforce, assuming either munitions jobs or temporarily replacing their husbands in the workplace. The economy grew in every sector. Farm output, as well as coal and oil production, rose dramatically. Railroads struggled to keep up as output rose from 13.6 billion loaded car miles in 1939 to 23.3 billion loaded car miles in 1943. The nation's spending rose too, as the government invested in the interstate highway system, schools, distribution of veterans' benefits, and new military technologies such as airplanes and computers.

The elation that overcame the country when the Japanese surrendered is forever epitomized in the image of a Silent Generation soldier pulling a young nurse to him for an impromptu kiss in the midst of the ecstatic Times Square crowd. World War II was over, and the US had emerged a superpower. The silents were all happy to lend the spotlight to their fathers, brothers, friends, and neighbors who risked their lives to save America; yet they were ambitious and eager to find success and stability.

The generation is small in number, as birth rates are naturally low during times of war and financial hardship. But in some ways, the title is a misnomer. The generation was silent in the sense that member cohorts largely conformed to accepted standards of behavior. At the same time, it was their willingness to conform that provided the unity necessary for peace and stability and then fueled the drive and teamwork the country needed to start rebuilding. As a child of silent parents, I believe author Bob Henger got it right when he described them as "quiet, industrious people who focused on getting things done," a bridge generation so consumed with their own survival and the well-being of their parents that they became "empathizers, mediators, conciliators, preferring cerebral approaches to problem solving over confrontations."[86]

When cohorts of the Silent Generation reminisce, they recall simple times when money was tight, but family ties were tighter; they recall how, together, families weathered the Great Depression and the horrors of WWII. Some of the oldest cohorts still remember the Japanese surprise attack on Pearl Harbor, and who can forget how the US answered by dropping the first atomic bomb on Hiroshima? After sixteen years of depression and war, the country was ready for peace and stability, and the silents were ready to lead the way.

Connecting with the Silent Generation

My dad, William (Bill) Slaughter, is from a small town in Arkansas. Even as a boy, he knew what it meant to work hard. When he was not at school, he was bagging groceries and pumping gas at his uncle's general store. It was the summer he worked in the boiler room at the local paper mill that he determined he would do more with his life. So with patriotism and the desire for peace and stability still well-ingrained in his generation, he set off to prep school at Marion Military Institute.

Before long, this young country boy (the first in his family to attend college) was awarded a congressional nomination from Senator John L. McClellan of Arkansas and was accepted into the United States Naval Academy. Loyal to his commitment and willing to sacrifice for the sake of the country, my dad served twenty years in the military as a fighter pilot and flight instructor. After completing his military duty, he worked for a defense contractor developing the new field of computer-based training for flight simulation. He worked there faithfully from nine to five until he suffered a heart attack and was forced into retirement.

My husband's parents share the same work ethic as mine. His dad drove a gas truck over the Boston Mountains in northwest Arkansas six days a week for thirty-eight years, and his mom never missed a day at the factory where she boxed fuses for forty-four years until her job and others like it were moved offshore where labor proved to be cheaper. Always considerate and generous, his mom is remembered for talking to anyone and everyone, and for continuously surprising people (from the neighbors to the school crossing guard) with little gifts just to brighten their day.

In many ways, my mom and dad's parenting style was authoritarian. We were expected to dust and vacuum our rooms once a week and pick up after ourselves every day. We addressed every adult with "yes, ma'am" and "no, ma'am," "yes, sir" and "no, sir," and we were prohibited from saying "shut up." There was a no-whining-allowed policy too. If we wanted something, we had the opportunity to make our case at the dinner table, and it was expected that the case would be logical and well rehearsed. When we gathered for the evening meal, the focus was on food and family. If the phone rang, it went unanswered. And the conversation revolved primarily around current world events and schoolwork. We were expected to bring home good grades, and it was simply understood that we would all go to college. The authoritarian parenting style found its balance though. We always received accolades for work well done, and there were lots of hugs and words of encouragement. We also had the freedom to choose our course of study and our vocation, as it was all about learning for the sake of learning, a concept that is disappearing today.

What my husband and I admire most about the Silent Generation is their steadfastness and trustworthiness. We could depend on them then and can still depend on them to keep their word and to stand true to their employers, churches, and families, to their beliefs, morals, and ethics. There is something quite comforting in knowing that right is right and wrong is wrong.

Baby Boomers

Birth Years	1946-1964
Formative Years	1946-1982
Age in 2016	52-70
Core Values / Characteristics	Optimistic, Confident, Career-Driven, Assertive, Ethical, Demanding, Rights Oriented, Competitive, Creative, Pay-Your-Dues Leadership, Personal and Deferred Gratification, Community/Group Involvement, Work as a Strong Element of Personal Identity, Argumentative/Challenging of Institutional Authority

The Name

Dramatic increases in industrial war production between 1945 and 1960, followed by an expansion of production for export, set the stage for The Golden Age of American Capitalism and the largest generation prior to ᴧennials—the baby boomers. There was never any question that ᗡ generation would be called the baby boomers, as 3.4 million babies were born in the United States in 1946, and approximately four million were born each year during the 1950s. By 1964, the baby boomer population had reached almost seventy-seven million.

The Historical and Social Context

Older boomers no doubt recall the sense of confidence that prevailed in the decades following the WWII victory and the subsequent economic surge. That confidence and the G.I. Bill compelled veterans to leave home in pursuit of advanced degrees and couples to flee decaying cities in search of safer, more affordable places to raise their families. Consumerism continued to grow as the American Dream to own a home, a few cars, and a TV set moved to suburbia. Suburbia was a uniquely American phenomenon that radically changed the American landscape politically, socially, and economically, as work life became distinctly separate from homelife and as culture grew increasingly homogenized.

Developers, some of them government funded, responded quickly to meet the housing demand. One such developer, William Levitt, led the way by creating cookie cutter communities known as Levittown— one in New York, one in Pennsylvania, and one in New Jersey. He streamlined construction by breaking it down into steps and training each group of construction workers on a single step, much like an assembly line. Initially, all the houses were built according to a single house plan and consisted of two bedrooms, one bathroom, and a kitchen situated at the back of the house in clear view of children playing in the backyard. Eventually, consumers were given other options. They could choose from a four-bedroom Cape Cod for $11,500; a three-bedroom, one-story rancher for $13,000; or a two-story colonial with three or four bedrooms for $14,000 and $14,500, respectively.[87]

The houses were fittingly arranged along curved streets, conspicuously different from the city grid design, and all were equipped with the latest appliances in white, gold, and, my favorite—olive green. "Between 1949 and 1969, the number of households in the US with at least one TV set rose from less than a million to 44 million. The number of commercial TV stations rose from 69 to 566. The amount advertisers paid the TV stations and networks rose from $58 million to $1.5 billion."[88] Car sales skyrocketed too. By 1960, 80 percent of American families had at least one car and 15 percent had two or more.[89] As white families began populating suburbia, much of the black community moved into the cities to assume new manufacturing jobs. While many argue that Levittown, and other communities like it, promoted conformity and racial segregation, others counter that the communities simply reflected the American culture at large.

The penchant toward innovation in the United States, sustained by extreme economic growth, enabled major achievements in the fields of science and medicine during the boomers' formative years. Some of those achievements include the following firsts:

- Electric power production from a nuclear reactor
- Detonation of a thermonuclear weapon
- Use of a heart and lung machine in surgery
- Supersonic flight
- The Salk polio vaccine administered in mass
- Transatlantic telephone cable
- Launch of the nuclear-powered submarine USS *Nautilus*

The competition between the two world superpowers also fueled advances in technology as the US and the USSR raced to achieve technological superiority, particularly as it related to space. The space race produced an array of technological benefits, from improved solar panels, implantable heart monitors, and improved computing systems, to water purification systems, light-based anti-cancer therapy, and global search-and-rescue systems. Space technology also produced popular spinoffs, such as scratch-resistant lenses, freeze-dried food, athletic shoes, Teflon-coated fiberglass, and the dustbuster.

The '50s brought opportunity and prosperity to many Americans, but the decade was not all *Leave it to Beaver* and *Father Knows Best* good times. These were also times of uncertainty and fear, as the relationship between the US and the Soviet Union had become tumultuous and tense. After the war, mounting instability and growing distrust ignited the long Cold War era (1945-1991). Although no shots were fired between the two competing superpowers, the countries were engaged in an ongoing series of political, economic, and military maneuvers.

It was democracy and capitalism versus authoritarianism and communism, a standoff that kept the world in a state of uncertainty and profoundly affected the everyday lives of the American people. Newspapers carried stories of UFO sightings, while science fiction films like *Invasion of the Body Snatchers* and alien threats from characters like The Blob were all the rage. Fear of nuclear attack prompted citizens across the country to build bomb shelters in their backyards and communities to conduct regular air-raid drills. And in their classrooms, teachers aired *Duck and Cover*, a ten-minute film that featured Bert the Turtle who showed children what you should do "when you see the flash."

Widespread fear of the spread of communism known as the Red Scare raged from 1947 to 1957. Concerns heightened when the House Un-American Activities Committee (HUAC) conducted a series of high-profile hearings alleging that communists disloyal to the US had infiltrated government, schools, the entertainment industry, and other areas of American life. Alger Hiss, a high-ranking State Department official was accused of espionage, convicted of perjury, and sentenced to forty-four months in prison. Julius Rosenberg and his wife Ethel were convicted of espionage and executed for passing information about the atomic bomb to the Soviet Union. A group of screenwriters known as the Hollywood Ten refused to cooperate at their hearing and were cited for contempt, given prison sentences, and blacklisted.

Joseph R. McCarthy used the HUAC hearings as a blueprint for his own anticommunist campaign in the Senate, a maneuver that made him a powerful and feared figure. McCarthy claimed to have a list of 205 State Department employees who were members of the Communist Party. His investigations against communist infiltration of government operations continued until he confronted the US Army. McCarthy's investigation proved fruitless, but the Army brought its own charges against the senator. The Army-McCarthy hearings dominated public television for months, exposing McCarthy's unethical tactics to approximately eighty million viewers. These hearings and several Supreme Court decisions brought an end to the Red Scare, as well as McCarthy's career.

The Cuban Missile Crisis was the most dangerous and direct confrontation between the US and the Soviet Union during the Cold War. On October 14, 1962, an American U-2 spy plane snapped photographs over Cuba, the first clear evidence that Soviets were building medium-range nuclear missile sites. When informed of the discovery, President John F. Kennedy immediately assembled a group of advisors who met secretly over the next week to consider options. Time was of the essence. According to intelligence, Soviet missiles could be in full operation within fourteen days. With Florida only ninety miles from Cuba, these missiles had the capability of striking major American cities, including Dallas and Washington DC. And each warhead had sixty times the destructive power of the atomic bomb dropped on Hiroshima.

On October 22, Kennedy ordered a naval quarantine around Cuba to prevent the Soviets from bringing more military supplies into the country. He also sent a letter to Soviet Premier Nikita Khrushchev demanding that the Soviets remove the missiles and destroy the sites.

That evening the President went on national TV to inform the public, emphasizing that should the Soviets fail to comply, the US would be forced to take military action.

A second tense week followed, and neither side backed down. Kennedy's course of action included a public pledge that the US would not invade Cuba if the Soviets withdrew their missiles, and a private ultimatum threatening to attack Cuba within twenty-four hours if the offer was rejected. On Saturday, October 27, Washington held its collective breath as the lives of one hundred million US citizens and more than one hundred million Soviet citizens lay in the balance. At this moment, the superpowers stood closer to nuclear annihilation than they ever had before or ever have since. At the last minute, Khrushchev accepted, and the crisis was resolved.

As the '60s progressed, the US became a hotbed of social activism and reform as people became increasingly concerned about people's rights. A myriad of social change initiatives erupted around the country, promoting civil rights, students' rights, and women's liberation, while Vietnam War protests raged in the background. In an attempt to fight injustice, people openly displayed their discontent on college campuses and elsewhere by participating in public marches, sit-ins, rallies, and petition drives, and burning bras, flags, and draft cards.

Why did social activism erupt in the US, and why did it do so in the '60s? For one thing, beginning in the '30s, the government had taken a more active role in people's lives by stepping in to help alleviate the impact of the Great Depression. Now people were beginning to look to the courts, to Congress, and to the president to protect them from social injustice too. Second, now that the US had assumed a global leadership role, it only seemed right that the government should practice what it preached and take care of its own. Furthermore, the country was experiencing an economic surge that made the socioeconomic gap more evident, and the affluent had more time and resources to commit to fighting social problems. Another factor that contributed to the social unrest was the size and impact of the youth culture. The generation was larger and more well off than ever before, and more youth were graduating from high school and going to college. "College campuses in particular teemed with young people who had the freedom to question the moral and spiritual health of the nation."[90]

Following the assassination of the young and popular President Kennedy and amidst the atmosphere of social unrest, a counterculture began to bubble up. This counterculture was made up primarily of middle-class, white baby boomer teens and college students who were on a mission to actively reject the norms of their parents, of the '50s, and of suburban conformity as a whole. These youth did not believe their parents' values were enough to help them come to grips with the social and racial issues of the '60s. These malcontents reacted by withdrawing from mainstream culture and by adopting the hippie lifestyle, displaying radical attitudes about drugs, sex, and communal lifestyles. The counterculture made up less than 10 percent of the American youth population, yet what we remember most about the culture in this era are the mini-skirts and suede knee-high boots, floral prints and tie-dye material, beads, flowers, and peace signs. In actuality, most young Americans supported the Vietnam War and sought careers and lifestyles similar to their parents.[91] The hippie lifestyle receded into the background when their cause became mainstream in the early '70s.

Connecting with the Baby Boomer Generation

A majority of baby boomers have reached retirement age now, but they (or *we* I should say) are determined to stay young and active. Many are going back into the workforce, where our work ethic is still valued. We are finding second careers, and sometimes making it more difficult for younger generations to find work. Boomers are known for their enthusiasm and strong work ethic but are also highly criticized for being selfish and materialistic. We are particularly at odds with Xers and millennials for having initiated programs that are proving to be unsustainable.

Boomers were born during the post-war economic boom to parents who were still riding the wave of opportunity and optimism; thus, we were raised with certain expectations about the future. Those of us born at the tail end of the generation are sometimes referred to as "jonesers." "Jonesin'" means "to crave or yearn for," and we are a generation known for trying to keep up with the neighbors. We were just coming of age when the long period of mass unemployment and deindustrialization hit and continued to plague the US during the '70s and '80s. So despite growth in the technology sector, fewer opportunities were available than anticipated. During the 2008 elections, *Newsweek* astutely characterized us as "residual '60s idealism mixed with the pragmatism and materialism of the '80s."[92] Thus, we have a unique connection with Xers, as we are more cynical than earlier boomers, and we share a life experience with millennials because in many ways we have felt unfulfilled too.

Like our children, jonesers are becoming increasingly distrustful of everything, from the government to the media. We miss having a church and a government we can count on in a country where the American flag is treated with respect. We miss the days that ended with, "And that's the way it is … [reads date]. This is Walter Cronkite, CBS News; good night." We listened to "The Star Spangled Banner" play, we heard the TV go to static, and we went to sleep confident we had the facts. Now we are barraged with information. At any time, we can go directly to a news source online for information, or we can download an aggregator app to get a customizable view of just the news and information we want. Plus, social networking sites and blogs provide the means of sharing and commenting on stories anywhere and at any time of day or night.

Getting the hard new is not simple like it used to be. Now the burden is on the consumer to distinguish between truth, opinion, and parody, if indeed those factors even matter any more.

And like Sam Hunt sings, my husband and I miss "Mama's prayers and Daddy's speech / Front porch philosophies" because we were "Raised on It." And although we were "a little too young and dumb to see" back then, we know now that those philosophies became a part of who we are. With the busyness of life—school, work, sports, clubs, music, social media, and so on—families do not sit on the porch or around the table and philosophize about life anymore. We lament having lost those one-on-one forums for sharing ideas with family and friends and are making efforts to create moments like those today.

Generation X

Birth Years	1965-1982
Formative Years	1965-2000
Age in 2016	34-51
Core Values / Characteristics	Self-Reliant, Skeptical, Distrustful of Marriage, Well Educated, Entrepreneurial, Inclusive, Individualistic, Pragmatic, Patient, Results Oriented, Distrustful of Organizations, Consider Education as a Means to an End and Survival More Important Than Loyalty

The Name

The name "Generation X" first appeared as the title of a 1950s Robert Capa photo essay that explored what it is was like to grow up immediately after WWII. The term was later popularized by Douglas Coupland in his 1991 novel of the same name about young adult lifestyles in the

1980s. Some contend that Coupland took the term from Billy Idol's band, Generation X. Regardless, what is significant here is that despite attempts to coin a more descriptive name like Echo Generation or Thirteenth Generation (since they are the thirteenth generation to be born in the United States), X is the name that stuck. Because of widespread availability of the pill, the legalization of abortion, and the increase in the number of women entering the workforce, Gen X is a smaller generation. Their size, plus the fact that they are named not for what they are but for what they are not (not boomers and not millennials), they tend to get lost. And because they feel outnumbered, instead of initiating change, they tend to step back and accept the status quo, waiting for their turn to take the reins.

The Historical and Social Context

The '70s were both troubled and troubling. In their youth, Gen Xers were exposed to a number of watershed incidents and scandals that left them significantly more cynical.

- The Vietnam War—This war lasted almost twenty years, and unlike WWI and WWII, it ended on a sour note. By the time the US pulled out, Americans were more divided over the war than ever. The conflict between North and South Vietnam had not been resolved, and Americans were experiencing widespread inflation due to massive wartime spending. Plus, veterans returned home only to face physical repercussions, as many were wounded and others suffered from exposure to Agent Orange. And there were psychological repercussions, as many Americans viewed returning soldiers as having killed innocent civilians or as having *lost* the war. The US negotiated a peace agreement with North Vietnam in 1973, and South Vietnam fell to the communists in 1975.

- A Vice President Charged with Tax Evasion—Spiro Agnew pleaded no contest when he was charged with bribery, conspiracy, and tax fraud. In exchange for his plea, the court dropped charges of political corruption, and Agnew was fined $10,000, sentenced to three years probation, and disbarred by the Maryland court of appeals. Agnew resigned on October 10, 1973.

- The Watergate Scandal—Five burglars from Nixon's Committee to Re-elect the President broke into the office of the Democratic National Committee. President Nixon, who was clearly involved, demanded that the FBI stop investigating and told his aides to cover up the scandal. A congressional committee approved three articles of impeachment, but before proceedings began, Nixon resigned on August 8, 1974.

- The Iran Hostage Crisis—To protect oil interests in the '50s, British and American intelligence services planned a coupe in Iran, which put Shah Pahlavi into power. The Shah proved to be a cruel dictator, and in 1979, revolutionaries overturned the government. Ayatollah Khomeini assumed control, and the Shah was exiled. Many Iranians resented American intervention in their country's affairs. So in 1979, when President James E. "Jimmy" Carter allowed the exiled Shah to receive medical care in the US, pro-Khomeini students ambushed the American embassy in Tehran and took sixty-six hostages. Carter's attempts at diplomacy failed, and his botched military rescue ended in the death of eight servicemen. It was not until President Ronald W. Reagan delivered his inaugural address that all the hostages were released after 444 days of captivity. The hostages were taken on November 4, 1979, and released on January 21, 1981.

Time and time again, the government had looked powerless in the face of conflict. By the time Carter's presidency came to an end, the idealistic dreams of the '60s had been dampened by domestic scandal and foreign policy turmoil. Citizens had grown weary of ineffective government policies, high taxes, and the mounting problems that faced aging cities, and they were moving to the Sunbelt, the area stretching from southern California across the South and into Florida. This '70s demographic shift of like-minded Americans gave rise to the New Right, a group of conservatives whose votes contributed to President Ronald W. Reagan's election. While Americans had looked to the government to intervene during the Great Depression, by the '80s they were eager to get the government out of their lives and out of their pocketbooks. The results of Reagan's economic policies were mixed, but the impact of the Reagan Revolution on the American spirit was positive. Despite a recession in 1982 and a stock market crash in 1987, by the end of the era, Americans still felt a renewed sense of opportunity, patriotism, and confidence.

The move to the Sunbelt represented a shift in attitudes. The Sunbelt offered new lifestyles in the warm climate, as well as new job opportunities, particularly in agribusiness, tourism, and technology. Advances in technology were beginning to offer conveniences and timesaving advantages previous generations had never imagined. Cable TV expanded viewing options, while the VCR provided flexibility in TV viewing times. And MTV revolutionized the recording industry by introducing video recorded music. And, of course, the American lifestyle would never be the same after the personal computer.

Young adults were no longer hippies in pursuit of peace and free love; they were yuppies (young urban professionals) seeking to climb the corporate ladder. And the drive to achieve success required the pursuit of money and power. This new mindset was played out on the small screen by characters like J.R. on the popular TV series *Dallas*, who said, "Don't forgive and don't forget. And do unto others before they do unto you," and by the Gordon Gekko character in the 1987 movie *Wall Street* who declared, "The point is, ladies and gentlemen, that greed, for lack of a better word, is good. Greed is right. Greed works."

By the end of the '80s, the passion for civil and social rights so evident in the '60s and '70s had shifted; the focus that was once on helping society was now on the pursuit of individual happiness and success.

Connecting with Generation X

My oldest son was born in 1982 at the cusp of the Millennial Generation. Because he has a September birthday, he started kindergarten young, so his peers are true Xers; as a result, he shares their values and characteristics. He has a pragmatic approach to life, relying more on reason than feeling, and is task and results oriented both at home and work. He has a slew of close friends (an urban tribe you might say), and though many of them live hundreds of miles away, they communicate regularly, support one another always, and get together as often as possible. By comparison, I can count the number of high school and college friends my husband and I have stayed in contact with on one hand!

Although my husband and I have been happily married for thirty-three years, and all of our parents celebrated golden wedding anniversaries, my son's exposure to the divorce epidemic in America left him cautious. He wanted to get it right too, so after seven years of dating, he was finally engaged and married. My son and practically everyone in his urban tribe choose to live in the city, a trend that we are seeing across the US as the post-WWII pursuit of a pastoral American Dream moves to small, mixed-use, urban communities characterized by diversity and walkability.

The Millennials

Birth Years	1983-2001
Formative Years	1983-2019
Age in 2016	15-33
Core Values / Characteristics	Optimistic, Enthusiastic, Close to Parents, Entitled, Confident, Tech Savvy, Inclusive, Diverse, Cocky, Individualistic, Team Oriented, Narcissistic, Entrepreneurial, Achievement Oriented, Want Instant Gratification

The Name

Generation Y, which naturally follows Generation X, quickly became known as the Millennial Generation (or millennials) because they were the last generation born in the twentieth century. Strauss and Howe officially coined the term in their 1992 book *Generations*, and this is the name these birth cohorts still prefer. The generation is huge. Based on Census Bureau data, Pew Research found that the number of millennials in the workforce surpassed all other generations in the first quarter of 2015.[93] According to the Population Reference Bureau, the current population size is not necessarily related to increased birthrates as was the case in the 1950s, but mostly to an influx of immigrants, which significantly increased the number of women of childbearing age in the United States.[94] Now "42 percent identify with a race or ethnicity other than non-Hispanic white, around twice the share of the Baby Boomer generation when they were the same age."[95] Thus, the Millennial Generation has become the most diverse in the post-war US.

The Historical and Social Context

President Reagan's negotiations with Soviet leader Mikhail S. Gorbachev and his cry for Mr. Gorbachev to "tear down that wall" spurred progress toward resolution of the Cold War. In an effort to strengthen the Communist Party, Gorbachev introduced the political, economic, and social reforms known as *perestroika* and *glasnost*. But within the rigid communist structure, these initiatives proved ineffective, and the economic conditions in the USSR worsened. People around the world watched in awe as events that changed the course of history followed in rapid succession. The Berlin Wall came down in 1989, and the East German government opened its borders. By the summer of 1990, new democratically elected governments had replaced all of the former communist regimes of Eastern Europe. By the end of 1991, the Soviet Union had dissolved into its component republics and ceased to exist—final confirmation of the US status as "the world superpower."

But the twenty-first century brought more trouble at home and more reason for heightened anxiety. Terrorists hijacked four planes on September 11, 2001. Two crashed into the World Trade Center, one hit the Pentagon, and the fourth crashed in a field in Pennsylvania. More than three thousand people were killed. President George W. Bush immediately announced the Global War on Terror:

> *The attack took place on American soil, but it was an attack on the heart and soul of the civilized world. And the world has come together to fight a new and different war, the first, and we hope the only one, of the 21st century. A war against all those who seek to export terror, and a war against those governments that support or shelter them.*

The US quickly linked the attacks to al Qaeda, a terrorist group that operated under the Taliban regime's protection in Afghanistan. During the first one hundred days after Bush's announcement, the US started building a worldwide coalition for the war, took action to freeze al Qaeda finances and disrupt their funding pipelines, and launched operation *Enduring Freedom*. After years of pursuit in the unforgiving mountain regions of Afghanistan, the US finally found al Qaeda leader Osama bin Laden. US Forces attacked the compound where bin Laden was hiding and killed him on May 2, 2011. A few months later, President Barack H. Obama began withdrawing US troops. On December 28, 2014, the US and NATO officially ended their thirteen-year combat mission with Afghanistan. However, the US and its allies must continue to fight terrorism to stop the advances of ISIS and other terrorist organizations that threaten our lives and our freedom.

During the Red Scare, security took precedence for a time over civil liberties. Once again, civil liberties are at risk. US citizens have accepted the fact that in the wake of 9/11 the world has changed forever. Now we must continually negotiate to what extent we are willing to sacrifice liberties and privacy for the sake of personal safety and national security. We have largely accepted being inconvenienced when we travel, for example, but we are still uncomfortable with allowing government surveillance of citizens as we conduct our everyday lives.

Another factor that increases the uncertainty of growing up today is that we live in an age characterized by greed and lust for power. Young people are entering into a workforce that oftentimes encourages the kind of arrogance that enables blatant corporate corruption. Take the Enron Corporation debacle, for instance. *Furtune* magazine named Enron Corporation "America's Most Innovative Company" for six consecutive years, yet clever but fraudulent accounting practices designed to keep stock prices high brought the multi-billion dollar energy company to its knees. For years, Enron cooked the books, and the former "Big Five" accounting firm, Arthur Anderson, covered it up. Harvard educated ex-Enron CEO Jeff Shilling is said to have fostered a culture where deal making trumped ethics and where bonuses and reviews were based on an employee's ability to make big deals. Twenty-one people were found guilty. In 2006, Skilling was sentenced to 288 months (later reduced to 168 months) in prison, and was required to compensate his victims for more than $41 million.

The collapse of Enron was devastating to tens of thousands of people and shook the public's confidence in corporate America.

— Robert Mueller

Things that have happened with Enron and companies like that, where they've squandered their employees' pension funds, I think it has brought a new level of anxiety. People don't feel like they can trust their employer.

— Mike Huckabee

In a world that is rapidly transforming into a global community increasingly dependent on technology, we are often unsure about what to expect and then surprised by what transpires; it is not surprising that many times we fear the worst. The anticipation with which people rang in the New Year and the new millennium is a good example. Experts anticipated that a date-related computer glitch known as the Year 2000 problem (Y2K) could result in a catastrophic, worldwide computer failure, as any device with a clock or calendar function was susceptible. Though many tried, no one could predict the full impact on businesses, employers, banks, or everyday lives. The US government encouraged companies and citizens to prepare. The government and businesses spent billions of dollars rewriting code. Citizens stocked up on supplies, and some went so far as to take their cash out of the bank.

My husband and I were returning from our son's soccer tournament in Tampa, Florida, to our home in Charlotte, North Carolina. Having had no time to prepare, we spent the night driving, wondering if at any minute the power grid might go out, leaving us in utter darkness on I-95, or whether flight systems might suddenly fail and cause airplanes to fall from the sky.

Though worldwide fears were real, they proved largely unwarranted. While there were some isolated computer issues afterwards, nothing catastrophic happened when the clock struck midnight.

I have no proof that the sun is about to rise on the apocalyptic millennium of which chapter 20 of the Book of Revelation speaks. Yet, it is becoming apparent to all of us that a once seemingly innocuous computer glitch relating to how computers recognize dates could wreak worldwide havoc.

— New York Senator Daniel Patrick Moynihan (April 29, 1998)

So, it seems, the simple life of days gone by are finished, and the complexities of modern life are here to stay. There is the fear of those elements in our lives, the details of which we cannot fully grasp (like Y2K as we approached the millennium). And there is the anxiety that accompanies the constant struggle for power, for as David F. Wells says, "Everything is about power. Everything is about control, manipulation, domination, using or being used for someone else's purposes."[96] And there is senseless violence:

- Nicole Brown Simpson and Ronald Goldman Murder—After being asked to surrender, O.J. Simpson led police on a car chase across LA freeways in pursuit of his white Ford bronco. The chase was broadcast on live TV around the world. A high-profile team defended Simpson in the widely publicized, eight-month trial. Simpson was acquitted.

- Attack on Olympic Figure Skater—US figure skating champion Nancy Kerrigan was clubbed in the knee with a police baton one month prior to the 1994 Olympics. Rival skater Tonya Harding's ex-husband and a co-conspirator planned the attack, which became known as "The Whack Heard Round the World."
- Columbine High School Massacre—Two high school seniors, Eric Harris and Dylan Klebold, opened fire killing twelve students and one teacher then committed suicide.
- Oklahoma City Bombing—Timothy McVeigh and Terry Nichols bombed a federal building killing 168 people and injuring more than 680.
- Boston Marathon Terrorist Attack—Motivated by extremist Islamic beliefs and the War on Terror, Chechen brothers Dzhokhar and Tamerlan Tsarnaev planted pressure cooker bombs at the finish line, killing three people and injuring 264.

And the list goes on:

- South Carolina Woman Drowns Her Two Sons
- Twelve Are Killed in Showing of Batman Movie in Colorado
- Rodney King Beaten by LAPD, Officers Acquitted
- Fifty-Five Killed, Two Thousand Injured in Riots
- Sandy Hook Elementary Tragedy, The Deadliest Mass Shooting at a High School or Grade School in US History, Leaves Twenty Children and Six Adults Dead
- Virginia Tech University Senior Shoots and Kills Thirty-Two People and Wounds Seventeen, The Deadliest Shooting Incident by a Single Gunman in US History
- And More

A natural response to a cultural climate that causes fear and anxiety is to become apathetic and to turn inward; thus, the hyperindividualism we are seeing today should come as no surprise. Millennials typically want to change the world, the world that directly impacts their own personal lives, that is. They are eager to purchase goods from companies that commit to giving back to the community. They are also interested in volunteering when they are passionate about a cause. And they are motivated when they can connect to the story or see the direct impact of the time, skills, or effort they contribute.

Connecting with Millennials

The paradigm shift in child development theory weighed heavily on boomer parents, who now considered it their duty to continuously praise their children, to relentlessly nurture and protect them, and to at least try and address as many emotional, physical, or educational needs as possible. Many even expected the community and schools to educate and entertain their children with the same level of dedication and enthusiasm. Highly concerned about our children's self-esteem, we showered them with praises and rewards, even for accomplishments that required little to no effort. And while those children are now self-confident, they often display signs of entitlement and narcissism. Boomers were originally labeled the "Me Generation," writes Twenge, but in retrospect they were just posers preparing the way for the millennials, who have elevated the importance of self to a whole new level.[97]

Taken to the extreme, such overly exuberant childrearing styles can and do result in what is known as "helicopter parenting," a parenting style that overly protective mothers and fathers use whereby they become so involved in their children's lives that they discourage independence. We have all heard the stories of parents managing their college-age children's class schedules and trying to enforce curfews from afar. Since independence is crucial to the normal maturation process, it is not surprising that studies show children of helicopter parents are "more depressed and less satisfied with life" and feel they have "less autonomy" and are "less competent."[98]

Many millennials are known to have gotten stuck in this emerging adulthood phase, wasting away their important identity-forming twenties. Millennials long to be successful adults but oftentimes are not sure how to get there. Let's face it, when you are young, you believe you are invincible. Now add to that invincibility a pair of well meaning but overly protective parents, and simmer them with the cultural trends of their formative years . . .

- The Dot-Com Craze
- The Supersize Years
- The Housing Bubble
- The Wall Street Boom

and you have the recipe for a generation of young people that is exceedingly and unrealistically optimistic. Though millennials have experienced many senseless atrocities in their young lives, they still do not feel vulnerable. While our cultural attitude toward our twenties has always been "something like good old American irrational exuberance," says Meg Jay in *The Defining Decade*, the cultural paradigms of the twenty-first century have elevated the level of unrealistic optimism, and thus the resulting naivety and devastation.[99]

Boomer parenting, which is now considered overparenting, is having an impact in the workplace. Millennials, who are accustomed to being rewarded and getting immediate feedback and who are comfortable interacting with people older than themselves, have trouble waiting a year for a raise or a bonus, and are impatient when tasks require months or years to complete. Plus, they have no qualms about approaching executive leadership with any ideas for improving the organization, which has been known to bewilder many a boomer CEO. On the other hand, boomers tend to apprentice millennials because they appreciate their eagerness, which means they overlook Xer coworkers who, while stepping back to wait for their turn, do not appear to have as much drive.

I always prided myself in raising independent children, yet I see in my millennials many of the characteristics used to describe the generation. I see the effects of high self-esteem generated artificially from within instead of naturally from without through trials, tribulations, and hard work. On a personal note, though I complained about giving every child a trophy, I did not take action to prevent or abstain from the practice. Plus, looking back, it might have been helpful to insist that Bryce get a job as a teenager. I also grieve when I watch him struggle with knowing how to move forward into adulthood and facing pressures of postmodern life, with readily available technology, information and choice overload, and extreme competition from what is now in every segment of the population.

I feel compassion for this optimistic generation in which even the smartest and most educated have to settle for jobs where they are underpaid and underemployed, a generation that is eager to contribute, but forced to settle. Even the American Dream has dimmed, as millennials struggle to pay rent and wonder if they will ever be able to own a home. And I feel guilty. Perhaps I should have been stricter. I could have made them do more chores like my good friend across the street. Or perhaps I could have taken them to more music lessons or I could have made them read more before going out to play. But in the end, would that have made much difference? Despite what part I did or did not play in the challenges my millennials face, the best I can do now is be part of the solution.

Generation Z

Birth Years	2002-Present (tentative)
Formative Years	2002-The Future
Age in 2016	0-14
Core Values / Characteristics	Potentially: Innovative, Creative, Entrepreneurial, Philanthropic, Tech Savvy, Security-Minded, Realistic

Generation Z is the first generation to spend their entire childhood immersed in technology. Even as preschoolers, these children use smart devices to play, communicate, and get information. Toys are even introducing them to computer programming concepts providing them with fun ways to practice coding. Gen Yers are native techies, but at this point, we can only speculate as to what that means.

It is likely that Gen Z adults will exhibit many millennial traits: innovation, creativity, entrepreneurship, and philanthropy, all from a global perspective. They have the capacity to be extremely smart too, if the US takes positive steps to improve the education system and brings America back into alignment in academic areas where we are currently falling short. According to recent tests administered by the Educational Testing Service to people between the age of sixteen and sixty-five in twenty-three countries, millennials score lower than other age groups and fall significantly behind other countries in literacy, practical math, and problem solving in technology-rich environments.[100] Researchers tend to think that Gen Zers will be more realistic than millennials, but it is early, and only time will tell.

Gen Z will undoubtedly adopt a name that reflects the massive advances in technology with which they grew up, their bent toward diversity, or perhaps their exposure to terrorism at an early age. Names that experts and marketers have suggested include Digital Natives,

Generation Like, the Selfie Generation, the Rainbow Generation, the 9/11 Generation, and Homelanders.[101]

A LOOK INTO THE FUTURE

A provocative approach to looking at how historical events, trends, and other phenomena have shaped each generation is embodied in the Mindset List. This annual list published by Beloit College describes what has "always" or "never" been true for a group of incoming college freshman. The informative and entertaining list captures the attitudes and expectations of students each year, thereby enabling the college to better prepare for new students. The college released the first list in 1998, and due to its increasing popularity, they have released a new list every year. Here are a few items from the class of 2018 list, or what we can expect has "always" been true for millennials born in 1996.[102]

- During their initial weeks of kindergarten, they were upset by endlessly repeated images of planes blasting into the World Trade Center.
- Meds have always been an option.
- Attending schools outside their neighborhoods, they gather with friends on Skype, not in their local park.

Below are a few items from the class of 2026 list, or what we can expect has "always" been true for Gen Zers born in 2008:

- As a result of the new MedChip implant behind the ear, any doctor or pharmacist with a handheld computer can pull up their health history and vital signs.
- With the elimination of SAT and ACT tests, they can gain an advantage by submitting their genetic maps with their college applications.

- Declaring it safer than aspirin, doctors have always prescribed marijuana for the slightest pain.

Tom McBride and Ron Nief, in their book *The Mindset Lists of American History: From Typewriters to Text Messages, What Ten Generations of Americans Think Is Normal*, predict:

> *To some degree the class of 2026 has itself turned more inward and has decided, in fair but not great economic times, to sample the pleasures of advanced new technology. Here the key is the almighty computer. The American culture of a century and a half ago longed to read books, magazines, and newspapers in order to imagine what the world might be like. A century ago dawned the age of the great personalities on radio, the cinema, and television. But none of that could come close to capturing the world as informed by the technology of 2026, which reflects a reality not so much represented as enhanced, not so much real as virtual.*[103]

WHY SOCIETAL CONNECTION MATTERS

We cannot leave societal disconnects unaddressed; the stakes are too high. Even though the world is growing smaller due to globalization and the technology boom, the problems just keep getting bigger and more complex. Yes, the millennials and Gen Xers were hit by a recession that tripped them up early on, but an economic downturn seems pretty manageable when compared to other problems with exponentially more severe implications; there is ISIS, for example, the new cold-blooded brand of terrorism we are fighting abroad, and the senseless gun violence that kills more and more innocent people within our own borders every year. We face new moral and ethical problems with technologies that seemed like science fiction not too long ago, technologies such as artificial intelligence, genetic engineering, and the widespread use of unmanned aerial vehicles.

And of course we have a long list of issues for which we have no resolution, big issues that threaten to destroy our children's financial security, including exorbitant healthcare costs, national debt that exceeds any this country has ever known (well over eighteen trillion dollars and counting), and a Social Security program that is expected to run out of money in 2033. There is little question that as we seek to pay for some of these competing programs, our defense budget will take a hit. This comes at a time when we not only face mounting terrorism, but other critical foreign relations pressures as well, including ongoing negotiations with Iran over nuclear weapons production and UN sanctions; the plea from the Ukraine for international support as a separatist movement threatens peace and the path to democracy; and heightened rhetoric between nations as one accuses the other of initiating an arms buildup in Europe.

From the Silent Generation and the boomers to the Gen Xers and the millennials, we have to be able to look at the problems, talk about them, and find solutions. Right now we are doing more finger pointing than we are listening and talking. Young people need to move beyond indifference and engage in the future—believe in something, know what they believe in, know how to articulate their beliefs, and make a difference now. At the same time, the older generations need to stop criticizing and start mentoring—remember what you believe in, make sure you know how to articulate your beliefs, and be committed to a life of continuous learning and knowledge sharing. We do not want to change the way people think, but we want to encourage people to think—to think about the big life questions that trouble us on the inside, to think about the big societal problems that trouble us from the outside, and to think about virtue and happiness from a perspective beyond the self. If we do not build a bridge of understanding across the generational abyss and break through the barriers to communication, there are bound to be major consequences. And the need is urgent, as boomers are already beginning to transition leadership positions to the next generations.

CHAPTER 8
THE SPIRITUAL DISCONNECT

I see many people die because they judge that life is not worth living. I see others paradoxically getting killed for the ideas or illusions that give them a reason for living . . . I therefore conclude that the meaning of life is the most urgent of questions.
— Albert Camus, *An Absurd Reasoning: Absurdity and Suicide*

What is the purpose of life? is a silly question.
— Richard Dawkins, *The Unbelievers*

We need a purpose. At a conscious level, that is what gets us out of bed in the morning. We get up because we have children to take care of, a job or activity to go to, a friend or spouse who needs us. Otherwise, we wonder, "What's the point?" At a subconscious level, a purpose is what we need to keep us going for the month, the year, the decade . . . to the end of our lives.

Materialists do not agree. They contend that the only thing we can believe in is what can be proven, and that the only thing that can be truly proven is matter. As early as the fifth and sixth century BC, people subscribed to the philosophy of materialism (or what was known as "atomism") asserting that the world is made up entirely of uncaused, invisible, and immutable atoms. According to this theory, atoms bounce off of one another or cluster together in different arrangements in an infinite void, and that is what produces the visible world as we know it. Atomism has reinvented itself several times over the course of history as advancements have been made in the field of science and technology, the atomic theory being the most recent adaptation. But at the core of philosophies based on materialism is the belief that everything boils down to the smallest particles in motion; even the senses are just a result of atoms from external objects striking against the sense organs. Materialists hold, therefore, that life has no meaning, and that being the case, there is no need to pursue questions about the purpose of the world.

I would argue that without a purpose, there can be no spiritual connection, and the spiritual connection is important because it goes deep into our hearts. The search for spirituality (or faith), I would argue, goes beyond an individual's thoughts and into the inner consciousness. Bryce, who finds hope in knowing that "the sun fell then rose again the next day as God intended," would, no doubt, agree.

I choose to use the term "inner consciousness" because it comes closest to conveying what I mean by "connect" and "disconnect." So what is consciousness? According to the dictionary, consciousness is the state of being aware—aware of our sensations, our thoughts, our surroundings, and so on. We encounter some things through physical experience; the attributes (like size, shape, and weight) that make up these types of experiences can be measured and agreed upon. We encounter the other things through personal experience; these attributes (like the joy of Christmas morning, the warm sand on the beach, and the colors of a sunset) cannot be conveyed. So how do we become conscious of our experiences? How do we come to know the orangeness of the orange in the sunset; our subjective, phenomenal experience of the sand on the beach that makes it different from anyone else's experience; what it is like to be a bat, an earthworm, or me? That is consciousness.

A materialist would say that mental states occur the same way physical states occur, as the result of certain arrangements of atoms, which leads us to believe that with more technological advancement, computers will be conscious one day. The question remains then: How can a physical brain, which is made only of material substances, give rise to conscious experiences? A Christian would hold to a dualist view that the mind and the body (consciousness and matter) are separate. The question remains then: How do the mind and the body interact? Perhaps the mind is like a theater where our senses and emotions are contents of our consciousness, and we are the audience. Or maybe consciousness is like a river where our senses and emotions simply flow one right after the other. Where then is the central location in the brain that the movie takes place or consciousness happens?

For millennia, philosophers and scientists have struggled with the concept of consciousness. Even in the twenty-first century as we are learning more about the human brain and the field of consciousness studies is thriving, experts say the question of how and why consciousness occurs is unsolvable. Regardless, what I am referring to when I say "inner consciousness" is the place where the spiritual connection takes place. In this sense, the inner consciousness is where Plato's True Being and True Self exist. It is where Aristotle's Substance attains its inherent Form. It is the essence of an idea. It is the way in which we discover the meaning of the world. It is the place where truth is knowable. It is the place of my identity. It is my soul.

MY JOURNEY TO SPIRITUAL CONNECTION

At the ripe old age of nine, I was searching for spiritual connection. As a young girl, I spent many a day sitting in the backyard under the big oak trees with my basset hound, Willie, talking with God. Once I got my hands on a version of the Bible I could understand, I took myself down to the big Southern Baptist church that sits prominently in the middle of the town's main thoroughfare and joined a Bible Drill class. As chance (or predestination) would have it, I was the only one to attend, which gave the drill coach the opportunity to share with me one-on-one what the Bible teaches about truth and salvation from sin—what I had been searching for in my backyard talks. I prayed the sinner's prayer and was soon baptized. I found my spiritual connection in Orthodox Christianity.

Ever since that day, I have been seeking to know who I am, to know who God is, and to build a healthy, fulfilling relationship with Him that will sustain me through the dark places and bring me the greatest awe-inspiring joy in the bright places. Like the boundaries that provided me with "a self to react against" in my formative years, the challenges and sometimes sufferings I encounter give me a force to react against too. It is in that search for ways to react, in the decision as to whether to move forward or wallow in pain, and in how I ultimately choose to respond, that defines me.

There have been times, particularly as a young adult, when I was caught up in the "what" and lost focus on the "how," a common phenomenon in this stage of life, I think, when we are driving to prove ourselves in the workplace and provide for and raise our families. As I tell my children, when I was their age I often lived in anticipation of the next potentially big thing: a sizable bonus, a big promotion, an exotic vacation. But in reality, what brings me the greatest joy are those little things I do not have to earn but that God provides and surprises me with, like the time that I was beginning to teach my grandson about hummingbirds using video on my phone, when to our delight, a hummingbird lit and took a long drink from the feeder nearby. As I have reminded myself over the years, it is not what I do; that is, it is not whether I am a training director, a project manager, an author, or a stay-at-home mom. It is how I approach the tasks at hand and how I live my life—striving to live a life of love, integrity, honesty, and generosity—that defines who I am. I have come to rest in this truth.

THE JOURNEY TO SPIRITUAL CONNECTION

Of course, we all have our own, unique spiritual journey, and you may or may not find a spiritual connection. But based on the positive outcomes of my personal experience, I hope that you will search and that you will find a spiritual relationship that is equally fulfilling—that you will reconnect.

I understand that the world has changed. Tradition, the conduit through which faith was passed down to prior generations, has been disavowed and rendered obsolete, so people seldom look to the past for meaning anymore. I get that. And when they look to the future, they may find that it is too "riddled with unpredictability" to supply meaning or purpose, which are critical to our spiritual and mental health. Consequently, many end up looking "within, to the self, to find meaning, rules, and fulfillment."[104]

A 2015 Barna Group study seems to suggest that this is the case. The study looks at "What Most Influences the Self-Identity of Americans?" The results show that for a majority of people, the two biggest influencers are family (62 percent) and nationality (52 percent). Religious faith comes in a distant third at 38 percent, followed by career (23 percent), and then locale. Barna Group asked respondents to comment on the degree to which each of these influencers contributed to their personal identities. Interestingly, those who self-identify as Christian but do not make faith a priority are likely to say faith does not account for much of their personal identity. In fact, Gen Xers and millennials are less likely than other generations to claim that any factor shapes their personal identity.[105] So what do you think people typically rely on to shape personal identity in this new, postmodern world? You guessed it—the self.

Looking strictly into self for meaning is something I would caution that we guard against. But the message is all around us. From self-help podcasts like "Helping Us All Find the Love Within," to songs like Alicia Keys's "Superwoman," we hear this message: To find happiness, look for truth within. Thanks to the self-esteem movement, we have instant access to all the ways we can learn to love ourselves just as we are—without faith. We can find comfort and encouragement in music by joining the Love Yourself Music website and streaming songs from one of the 172 different "love yourself playlists," or find self-help strategies by entering "love yourself" in the Google search field and delving through the 242 million items in the result list.

Do not get me wrong. I know that to be healthy, we must love and accept ourselves. In God's instruction to "love your neighbor as yourself,"[106] there is the assumption that we should love ourselves, and, the Scripture goes on to say we should do so because we are "fearfully and wonderfully made" in his image.[107] But overemphasis on loving ourselves can prevent us from recognizing our own limitations. It can prevent us from getting to the point where we are "wrecked" as author and millennial Jeff Goins would say—where we are at the bottom and looking inward and upward, and not just inward for truth. As theologian and author David F. Wells points out, "It is the loss of confidence in ourselves that is the bedrock of the condition for growing confidence in God."[108]

The media relentlessly broadcasts an alluring yet corrupt version of the God Within message. The message that we have looked within and have spiritually connected with a living God in faith and that we are building a purposeful relationship with Him is a positive one. The message that threatens the prospect of finding a meaningful spiritual connection is the amalgamation of the ideas that 1) the self is the center of one's own universe, and 2) that the spiritual connection lies within. The result is a glorification of the self; it is not a relationship at all. As Søren Kierkegaard said in *Fear and Trembling*, ". . . he who loves God without faith reflects on himself, while the person who loves God in faith reflects on God."[109]

How disappointing it would be to find that God is no bigger than our own little world. As Ross Douthat points out in *Bad Religion*, that is the heresy of the message in books and movies such as *Eat, Pray, Love*. The story suggests that we can find divinity and truth by listening to the voice of God, which (conveniently) is actually our own voice within. Billions of us heard that same type of spiritual advice when we listened to guests of *The Oprah Winfrey Show* or even today when we turn on *The View*. Douthat expounds on the prevalence of the heretical "God Within" perspective:

> *It's the religious message with the most currency in American popular culture—the truth that Kevin Costner discovered when he went dancing with wolves, the metaphysic woven through Disney cartoons and the Discovery Channel specials, and the dogma of George Lucas's Jedi, whose mystical Force, like Gilbert's God, "surrounds us, penetrates us, and binds the galaxy together."*[110]

Maybe, like me, you watch these TV shows and movies, and when they are over, you feel uneasy. The overall message seems innocent enough, but there is something wrong. Hooray for us; we are being discerning. We are being attentive to underlying messages in the world that threaten to undermine our faith, messages that "shape us without us really knowing what they are."[111] The bottom line is that we have to be informed, educated, and aware of what we believe so that we are prepared to accept or reject the volumes of messages that bombard us every day as filtered through our personal belief system.

One truth I know for sure is that science cannot prove that God does not exist and theology cannot prove that He does. Chances are you struggle with the relationship between faith and reason. That is not surprising, as the relationship has been fickle. In the days of Greek and Roman philosophers, they were one and the same. Later they became allies: belief came first followed by reason, reason helping to promote the understanding of belief. Finally, around the time of the Enlightenment, they became enemies, and that is how many people see the relationship today. But like the relationship between the mind and the body, we still lack an understanding of how the mind and the soul interact. The dawn of the twenty-first century and the genesis of a new mindset opened up the possibility of entertaining different intellectual approaches and different cultural paradigms. Now we can look at faith and reason as separate but equal. In the complexity of postmodernism, there exists the potential for extreme anxiety, yet there also exists a newfound freedom to embrace the paradoxical.

One should not think slightingly of the paradoxical, for the paradox is the source of the thinker's passion, and the thinker without a paradox is like a lover without a feeling: a paltry mediocrity . . . The supreme paradox of all thought is the attempt to discover something that thought cannot think.

— Kierkegaard[112]

As an intellectual who aspires to live a rich spiritual life, I choose reason *and* faith.

Another truth I know for sure is that even if you do not believe in God, you believe in something. So I encourage you to take the journey to establish or validate your belief system. Go into your internal consciousness where you wrestle with big life questions, to the place where you have internalized what you have been able to ascertain through reason; then be willing to acknowledge your emotions, for as nineteenth-century theologian Charles Haddon Spurgeon says in his defense of emotions, they are:

> . . . *our indispensable tool for navigating, for feeling our way through, the much larger domain of stuff that isn't susceptible to proof or disproof, that isn't checkable against the physical universe. We dream, hope, wonder, sorrow, rage, grieve, delight, surmise, joke, detest; we form such unprovable conjectures as novels or clarinet concertos; we imagine. And religion is just a part of that, in one sense. It's just one form of imagining, absolutely functional, absolutely human-normal.*[113]

Then take a leap of faith!

THE DISCONNECT WITH THE CHURCH

Faith is personal. It is a relationship we establish and nurture with God. In a metaphysical sense, Christians are part of the Global Church. In a physical sense, we can choose to be part of the local church, and the Bible encourages us to do so. The local church is the institution where we can go to learn more about our faith, worship God in community with others, serve God and others, and fellowship—all in an effort to grow our faith. Pew Research survey results demonstrate that there is a spiritual disconnect with the local church in America and that the disconnect is growing. A 2015 survey of 35,000 Americans found that in just seven years (2007-2014) the religious landscape changed significantly:

- The percentage of adults (ages 18 and older) who describe themselves as Christians has dropped by nearly eight percentage points, from 78.4 percent to 70.6 percent
- The percentage of Americans who are religiously unaffiliated (atheist, agnostic or "nothing in particular") has jumped more than six points, from 16.1 percent to 22.8 percent
- The share of Americans who identify with non-Christian faiths has risen 1.2 percentage points, from 4.7 percent to 5.9 percent
- Growth has been especially great among Muslims and Hindus[114]

This disconnect is trending upward, following a path that most European nations and Canada have been taking for some time now—the path toward secularism. Francis Spufford, author of *Unapologetic* (2013) explains: "In Britain, where I live, recent figures suggest that about 6 percent of the population goes regularly to church, and it's a number that has drifted steadily downward over the past few decades, while the average age of churchgoers has just as steadily trended upward: presently the average worshipper is fifty-one years old."[115]

According to a 2012 Gallup Poll, 40 percent of Americans attend church regularly and say religion is important in their lives. Although Americans continually report this level of religious belief, recent data indicate that the numbers do not support their claims.[116] "There is a persistent gap between the number of people who claim to go to worship services and the number who can actually be counted in pews."[117] Based on research from the Institute of Religion, the actual number of regular churchgoers is closer to 20 percent. Why the gap?

Spufford suggests that it is because Americans still believe that it bodes well for us and for our success to say we attend church. "The idea of people pretending to be regular churchgoers because it will make them look virtuous—or respectable, or serious, or community-minded—is completely bizarre to us," he writes. The British would rather say they do not go to church even when they do to spare themselves the embarrassment. I fear American attitudes about religion are not far behind our friends across the pond; our behavior is changing, which indicates a change in thought and attitude, so I suspect we are on our way down this path if we do not take action to redirect. In the meantime, evangelists are turning their sights toward developing countries, such as Africa, Asia, and the Arabian Peninsula, where people are more open to the Gospel message.

The church has been trying to resolve the faith disconnect since the beginning of modernity. After World War II, classical evangelicalism was flourishing. Mainline denominations were growing, and a new interest in Christian scholarship and education was becoming increasingly evident. By 1976, one-third of the country claimed to be "reborn." There was consistency in Protestant church tenets that held to the formal and material principles of the Reformation regarding Scripture and justification: "The Bible is God's revelation of truth and, as such, is authoritative in all matters of faith and conduct and that Christ, in his substitutionary death on the cross, is the only way to salvation entered into by grace alone through faith."

As the seeds of postmodernism began to sprout and grow, however, Evangelicalism faltered, and as the doctrinal boundaries faded, the theology weakened, and the church began to look more like a business or a psychologist's office than a place of worship, with all its strategies for attracting consumers and therapeutic tools for finding inner peace and self-satisfaction. "In a period of but a few years, it was decided that there was no longer any genuine truth, only truths; no principles, only preferences; no grand meaning which is outside of ourselves . . ."[118]

One of many recent surveys asking people to identify why they do not attend church elicited some of the same old feedback: "They don't want to be lectured, and they view the church as judgmental, hypocritical, and irrelevant."[119] As I have walked with Jesus over the years, and as I have read the Bible and other religious texts, I have determined that judgment and hypocrisy come part and parcel with the salvation deal. Until Christ comes again, the church will be made up of saints who are sinners but repent from their sins, and posers who claim to be saints but are actually false prophets. "Let both grow together until the harvest," Jesus said in the parable of the weeds.[120] Until the Day of Judgment, it is our job to discern the difference. Through my travels around the US, from Maine to Texas and Florida to Colorado, and in foreign countries from Africa to the UAE and from England to Turkey, I have come to realize that the Church does not have a monopoly on judgment and hypocrisy. Being judgmental and hypocritical are universal behaviors and totally characteristic of the human experience.

But let me reiterate, we must be discerning. Good and evil, right and wrong exist in the world, and we cannot simply turn our heads to what is evil and wrong. There is nothing inappropriate about actively assessing whether something is right or wrong. This kind of judging is neither narrow-minded nor self-righteous; it is a necessary process of articulating our own morality and building our own belief system. I admit that in my pride I occasionally make the mistake of going beyond the bounds of appropriate observation and discernment into the realm of criticism and condemnation. I suspect we all have, and we should be cautious to guard against that behavior. At the same time, we need to claim our right to differentiate between right and wrong without being labeled hypocrites, and as we mature, we should focus on learning how to talk about morality and ethics in ways that are encouraging and inoffensive.

How about the argument that people are leaving the church because they find the institution irrelevant? As my wise thirty-year-old niece says, "Truth is truth." People will either seek truth or they won't. There is no need to dress it up. Perhaps, as one Christian blogger suggests, "It isn't simply secularism or atheism that is drawing away people who were raised Christian, it is the search for definitive truth that is attractive too."[121] Unchurched Christian millennials, who make up only 15 percent of the unchurched population, are leaving the church as they become disillusioned by the institution's attempts to draw them in, not by offering truth in more authentic ways, but by appealing to their carnal nature—their desire for good lattes, hip praise bands, and pastors in jeans. While some find their way back to the church, particularly as they begin having children of their own, many discover new ways outside the church walls of making an impact on the fallen world.

Typically, unchurched Christians are convicted; they know their own minds and they are committed to their faith. As Thom Rainer and his son Jess explain in their book *The Millennials: How to Connect to America's Largest Generation*, millennial Christians are serious about their faith. They want to hear the Bible taught with depth and conviction, and they are committed to serving as missionaries wherever they happen to go.[122] Rachel Held Evans, a millennial cusper and a Christian, shares a poignant description of what her generation is looking for in a church:

> *We don't want to have to choose between science and religion or between our intellectual integrity and our faith. Instead, we long for our churches to be safe places to doubt, to ask questions, and to tell the truth, even when it's uncomfortable. We want to talk about the tough stuff—biblical interpretation, religious pluralism, sexuality, racial reconciliation, and social justice—but without*

predetermined conclusions or simplistic answers. We want to bring our whole selves through the church doors, without leaving our hearts and minds behind, without wearing a mask.[123]

Jonathan Aigner is another millennial who grew up Christian but is looking for a more traditional worship experience in a crowded, heavily consumer-focused church marketplace. Do away with the contemporary worship service, Jonathan advises in his blog; the experiment did not work. "Don't give us entertainment, give us liturgy," he adds, and "don't target us. . . . We need to look into the faces of old and young, rich and poor, of different colors, races, and ethnic backgrounds, so we can learn to see Jesus in faces that don't look like us." And finally, be willing to "welcome the toughest, deepest, grittiest, most desperate, most shocking questions." Aigner writes in his blog:

Week after week, season after season, year after year, let us participate in the drama of the gospel. It's not supposed to be fun. It's not supposed to produce intense emotional response. It's a microcosmic, disciplined, anticipatory remembrance of who we were, who we are, and who we are to be. We need this. We need these heartfelt rituals in our lives to keep us returning to the fount of grace, to mark our way back home.[124]

Well said, millennial Christians! Maybe we need to turn our focus on presenting the truth plain and simple and do away with all the folderol.

Then there are the non-Christians. Most young non-Christians have been exposed to some aspect of Christianity sometime in their lives. In response, many either decided that Christianity is not for them, or they determined that the quest is too difficult and time consuming to pursue; others simply do not have the tools they need to explore their options. So they are settling for happiness—not a happiness achieved through living a virtuous life, but through living a self-fulfilled life; not a happiness defined by the good life, but by a happiness defined by the trappings of success. There has been a "significant attitudinal shift with the 85 percent non-Christian Millennials. Their attitude toward Christians and churches is largely one of indifference."[125] So non-Christians make up the largest percentage of unchurched in America, and they pose the biggest challenge to reconnecting because indifference is an attitude that is exponentially more difficult to change than disillusionment.

So can non-Christians learn how to go beyond the self, to look inward *and* upward for truth, from the church? Wells explains how it looks when "the rearrangement of meaning around the self has entered into the church."

> *This rearrangement of meaning around the self, around its moods, needs, intuitions, aches, and ambiguities, has entered the church. Its presence is signaled wherever there are those who think, or act, as if the purpose of life is to find ways of actualizing the self, realizing it, and crafting it through technique or purchase, instead of restraining it out of moral considerations and in this sense putting it to death. Where Christian faith is offered as a means of finding personal wholeness rather than holiness, the church has become worldly.*[126]

"It is surely a great irony," says Wells, "that what evangelicals have most surrendered in the hope of becoming culturally relevant, is what, in fact, now makes them culturally irrelevant."[127] Give us unmasked conviction, says Evans. Give us heartfelt ritual, says Aigner.

Over the course of my lifetime, I have confronted judgment and hypocrisy in the church, as everyone does. Despite my social and spiritual maturity, I was denied the opportunity to go on a mission trip because I was one year too young. Despite my experience and faithfulness to teaching children over the years and commitment to Bible drills, my position as coach was filled by someone with more money and influence. Despite my master's degree in English and teaching experience, my application to teach English in China for the summer was declined because I had not tithed enough. My application to put my master's degree I earned with honors to work as an English teacher in the church school was denied; the kids loved me, but apparently the administration did not.

As we moved from place to place following job opportunities, we looked for churches where the pastor did not speak down to us, where the music was current but reverent, and where the Bible was the single source of truth. Some churches we visited were tolerant of everything, which left the gospel message watered down and uninspired. Others were excessively legalistic, which left me feeling awkward, as if I were part of a cult, not a congregation. The megachurches with moving lights, fog machines, rock bands, and promises of physical healing scared me away. One church that we attended for years became so large and powerful, with all of its satellite churches, and strayed so far from its original biblical message that I could not bare to sit through an entire service. When people began leaving, the renowned preacher raged from the pulpit that anyone who abandoned the church would be condemned to hell. Wow.

Have I had some positive experiences in the church in my pursuit of truth? Yes. Have I found a church where I can truly worship? No. Do I continue in my personal walk with Jesus? Absolutely. That is because the church is the institution conceived by God but established and operated by fallible mankind. Faith, on the other hand, is what exists outside of the physical world and is lived out in relationship with a personal God.

WHY SPIRITUAL CONNECTION MATTERS

When I look at how societal context has been shaping internal consciousness during my lifetime, what I see is that young people growing up in the Age of Anxiety are searching for knowledge and truth that will introduce some stability and certainty into their lives. As the world grows smaller and more connected, yet increasingly complex and more isolating, young people are looking for a safe place where they can come as they are and ask tough stuff. We need to create that place.

Jesus, friend of sinners, the one who's writing in the sand
Made the righteous turn away and the stones fall from their hands
Help us to remember we are all the least of these
Let the memory of Your mercy bring Your people to their knees
Nobody knows what we're for only what we're against when we judge the
*   wounded*
What if we put down our signs crossed over the lines and loved like
*   You did*

Oh Jesus, friend of sinners
Open our eyes to world at the end of our pointing fingers
Let our hearts be led by mercy
Help us reach with open hearts and open doors
Oh Jesus, friend of sinners, break our hearts for what breaks yours[128]

PART 3

A FRAMEWORK
FOR ACTION

CHAPTER 9

RECOVERY AND PREVENTION

To be what we are, and to become what we are capable of becoming,
is the only end of life.
— Robert Louis Stevenson, *Familiar Studies of Men and Books*

I t was not so long ago that mental illness was considered incurable, and people diagnosed with a severe disorder were forced to spend their lives locked away in pain and isolation. The large asylums that operated between 1850 and 1950 served to propagate the belief in the incurability of these conditions. After this one-hundred-year period, pharmaceutical companies began introducing medications, and some patients were able to return to their communities; but recovery was limited, as most practitioners continued to believe that mental patients could never be fully functioning.

Around the turn of the century, research began to demonstrate that people who suffer from mental illness can be independent, and patients started advocating for services. The Bush administration listened, so in 2002 President George W. Bush established the New Freedom Commission on Mental Health, and by 2003, the commission claimed recovery as its overarching goal. An APA article regarding the commission's 2003 report, "Achieving the Promise: Transforming Mental Health Care in America," concludes that "the nation's mental health system was broken and identified the major flaw as the lack of a vision of recovery."[129]

WHAT IT MEANS TO RECOVER

In 2002, the National Alliance on Mental Illness (NAMI) published a research study of people who have lived with a whole range of psychiatric disabilities. In doing so, they captured common themes on the topic of recovery. It is unusual to read a description of what people who are truly suffering feel, rather than how experts perceive they feel. People who suffer from mental illness described recovery as:

- The reawakening of hope after despair
- Breaking through denial and achieving understanding and acceptance
- Moving from withdrawal to engagement and active participation in life
- Active coping rather than passive adjustment
- No longer viewing oneself primarily as a mental patient and reclaiming a positive sense of self
- A journey from alienation to purpose
- A complex journey
- Not accomplished alone—it involves support and partnership[130]

According to the NAMI, "recovery from serious mental illness is not only possible, but for many people living with mental illness today, probable."[131] While the message in this report was positive, the concept of recovery from mental illness had not yet filtered down into the institutions of learning devoted to the education of mental health professionals, and certainly not to the general public.

In its 2006 National Consensus Statement, SAMHSA defined "recovery" as "a journey of healing and transformation enabling a person with a mental health problem to live a meaningful life in a community of his or her choice while striving to achieve his or her full potential." By 2009, the vision had not gotten enough traction to elicit significant changes in mental health treatment, so SAMHSA acquired government funding and initiated a five-year plan to expand its recovery-centered approach. In partnership with the APA and four other mental health organizations, SAMHSA launched the Recovery to Practice (RTP) initiative. The organizations are working together to provide resources and training for mental health professionals and the mental health community at large, including patients and their families. The online resource database includes articles, stories, videos, and case studies that address questions about what recovery is and how to implement recovery-oriented practices in support of those who are pursuing recovery. The training materials are said to be "relationship based, emphasizing the healing context in which specific services should be delivered; person centered, embracing the whole person (not just the illness or pathology), and encouraging that individual to achieve his or her life goals; hopeful; and strengths based."[132]

The effort to integrate the concept of recovery into the mental health care system is underway, and the message of the recovery movement is just beginning to enter into the public conversation. But progress is slow. Bryce and I never sensed that mental health professionals were collaborating or that anyone was eager to look at Bryce's condition holistically. However, there are early signs that we can break through the stigma as an increasing number of people are stepping out to share their stories. As one *New York Times* science reporter, Benedict J. Carey, says in his 2011 series "Lives Restored," "An increasing number of them [people who suffer from mental illness] are risking exposure of their secret, saying that the time is right."[133] And that is important. Because as Brandon Appelhans, a seminary student with bipolar disorder puts it so eloquently: "If we keep our stories to ourselves, they die there."[134]

A DISEASE IS A DISEASE, OR IS IT?

We can start with the work accomplished within the medical community to date to build a stronger foundation from which to better drive change. Other private initiatives to support a more optimistic view of recovery are also growing. The Kennedy Forum, for example, is on a mission to "revolutionize the way mental health care is delivered in America and create a future where diagnosis and treatment covers the brain and the body."[135] And the Jed Foundation is actively working with colleges and universities to promote emotional well-being and mental health programming, reduce substance abuse, and prevent suicide on our nation's campuses.[136] So why can we not think of mental disorders in the same way we think of physical diseases?

Having a mental illness is "really no different than if you have a heart attack or another chronic illness," says Mary A. Jansen, PhD, member of the APA Recovery Advisory Committee. "Once you recover from the acute stage, you generally begin a recovery process, with a team of professionals and interventions all working toward helping you get back to the highest level of functioning you can achieve." A recent article about the Recovery to Practice initiative further explains Jansen's position:

In the same way that cardiologists might encourage heart attack patients to stop smoking, start exercising and work on lowering their cholesterol, she says, psychologists and others committed to a recovery-oriented approach now use psychosocial rehabilitation interventions to assist people with mental health conditions. These services . . . are designed to involve individuals in a partnership with professionals as they try to gain—or regain—a meaningful life, however they define it.

That recovery-oriented approach shouldn't just be used with people who have severe depression, schizophrenia, bipolar disorder and other serious mental illnesses . . . It's also useful for any mental health condition that keeps someone from functioning as well as he or she could.[137]

Consider Bryce, for example. He has recovered. He is managing his OCD, anxiety, and depression in much the same way I manage my herniated disks and breast cancer, by recognizing and owning the problem, creating a support system, educating himself, advocating for himself, and then developing and executing a self-help plan that enables him to set and progress toward his short- and long-term goals.

I completed the original physician-driven recovery plan, which included a neurologist who diagnosed and monitored the herniated discs; a chiropractor and a physical therapist who treated them; and a pain management physician who prescribed medication. Over time, I was able to wean myself off of all the medication and do the physical therapy at home. My self-help plan now includes regular exercise, a sensible diet, as well as regular checkups and health screenings. And I avoid extremely negative stress situations like the sexual harassment and retaliation I experienced previously.

Similarly, Bryce is developing a self-help plan of his own, which he explains in his own words:

Managing my mental health is about changing my mindset and behaviors, and that takes patience and time to reflect. For me, it's about getting a better understanding of reality. There is no magic pill. Sometimes that means putting myself in difficult situations to figure out who I am and how to be happy.

I have already adopted a few strategies that help. I keep daily logs, for example. The logs track my medicine dosages, shifts in behavior, and life events. I am encouraged when I look back through my logs and see a history of improvement. A glance at how I improved from month to month boosts my spirits and jolts me out of those short rollercoaster rides of depression.

My fiancée helped me recover from my anxiety by giving me love and support in moments when I had an urge to rush to the mirror to look at my skin. She helped me change my behavior by encouraging me to generate positive thoughts or to engage in activities that reduce my stress and distract me from picking at my skin. She continues to encourage me by sharing positive thoughts that help prevent panic attacks. For example, she tells me that she loves me for my heart and strong character. "People with oily skin are less likely to have a lot of wrinkles when they get older," she says. If those positive thoughts don't work, she takes me to the steam room or sauna so that I can do some breathing exercises. So one thing that helped me recover was having love in my life from someone who could support me as I stood in the mirror and cried as I picked at my face.

Talking to those who support me helps too. There are essentially two perspectives that influence me. My mom and my fiancée have one perspective; they tell me what I'm doing wrong. When I'm feeling sad, they say, "Here's the problem." They don't sugarcoat it. Sometimes it is hard to hear, but you need these people. Then there is Dad. Dad is soothing. He doesn't try to change my mindset; he is

just there in every way. Dad empathizes with me. He tells me stories
about how he made it through difficult times. When someone tells
you stories, it's inspiring. You need both perspectives.
In the end, however, you have to be the one to decide to change.

Bryce and I have talked to and read about other families who face
mental health diagnoses with symptoms that are much more debilitating
than Bryce's. As scientific evidence indicates, they can recover too. Matt,
for example, is a twentysomething who has been diagnosed with bipolar
disorder. On the road to recovery, Matt is eager to share his optimism
and wants people to know that there is hope.

Matt started seeing a difference in himself as he transitioned from
high school into college. "Out on my own, feeling naïve, not sure how
to take the world, the stress built up. I experimented with drugs, but not
too many, and I drank a lot." As a sophomore and junior, Matt battled
with some physical illnesses, one being shingles, which experts believe is
stress related. His grades fell to the point where he could not stay on his
degree path, but still eager to succeed, he transferred to a school closer to
home. There he attended classes and worked a job but was still drinking.
After experiencing several psychotic breakouts, Matt agreed to seek help.
At that point, psychiatrists diagnosed him with bipolar disorder. "It was
a dark time. It was tough, and I was tired. I didn't know what to do. I
took the meds the doctors gave me, but I didn't know what was going
on. I was still going to school, but I was sedated. I had delusions, and it
was scary. I realized I could really lose myself."

Determined to hang on to his identity and not "just be that guy
that's bipolar," Matt buckled down and focused on doing work. He and
his dad spent long hours getting a business up and running, and Matt
is currently working with a team to build the operation. "Sometimes it's
hard to get up in the morning; it's hard to be motivated," Matt admits,
"but I don't blame things on the condition. I am no different than

anyone else. Everyone has problems. I'm in a good situation and am taking advantage of what I have. I am going to keep it up and do the right thing."

When asked what suggestions he would have for someone who is experiencing mental health challenges like his, Matt said, "I recommend that you try to learn about yourself, what you are capable of and who you are, and understand that people who are close to you and love you are there to help. You need to reach out to them." Matt also stresses the importance of taking care of your mind and body. "Keep studying and exercising. Build some strengths. These are hard meds, and it's difficult, but you can recover. Have some discipline, have love and support, don't isolate yourself, and try to make an effort."[138]

Based on the definition, Bryce and I have recovered, Bryce from a mental illness and me from a physical one. We are both living meaningful lives in community with others as we seek to achieve our full potential, he in his way, me in my way, and each in support of the other. Matt too has recovered and is finding his place in the world.

EMBRACING RECOVERY AND PREVENTION

So why can we not think of mental disorders in the same way we think of physical diseases? I believe that this question lies at the root of the stigma problem and the answer goes back to the definition of recovery and our inability to embrace the definition as a society. No doubt there are a multitude of reasons why, but one is that scientists know less about the brain than they do about any other organ in the body; the brain is complex and mysterious. "A human brain weighs nearly three pounds (one and a half kilograms) and consists of more than a billion neurons (nerve cells), with many billions of interconnections. Out of all these connections come our extraordinary abilities: perception, learning, memory, reasoning, language, and—somehow or another—consciousness."[139] Oftentimes what we do not understand, we fear. The more we talk about a concept, however, the more we understand it, and eventually we hone the definition and come to an agreement.

My call to action speaks to the cause at a fundamental level. My concern is with driving the message of recovery and prevention home at the level at which people seek self-identity and achieve societal and spiritual connection. Right now this conversation is largely taking place on social media, which is ironic, since the Internet is renowned for its potential to damage the self-identity of those who post there. In this public space, those suffering from anxiety and depression seek answers in blogs, on networking sites, and in chat rooms where it is virtually impossible to differentiate healthy answers from unhealthy ones, and where personal stories of pain and struggle can be lost in a sea of information. Or the opposite can occur; instead of getting lost, the story can be sensationalized. In the world of virtual reality making, competition, and one-upmanship, stories can end up spreading myth and misinformation. That is the kind of outcome that threatens to damage the recovery movement and the momentum for change that is underway.

What young people need are real relationships grounded in the real world. Long-term intergenerational relationships can provide an effective vehicle for filtering through the noise that technology and the Information Age impose. Definition derives from public conversation, and the best place for public conversation to begin is in one-on-one dialogue that takes place where we live, where we work, and where we worship. Intergenerational relationships, in particular, can enable a means of constructing missing boundaries, creating strong identities, and enforcing the sense of self that young people need to be successful and fulfilled. Their mentoring partners, in turn, can reap the benefit of having relationships that infuse them with renewed meaning and purpose and encourage a reassessment of values and belief systems. It seems to me that this communication piece is missing from the current strategy to stop the stigma. What we need are the right tools for having the right conversations at the right time with the right mentor and mentee relationships.

Clearly, the mental illness recovery phenomenon is multidimensional and difficult to navigate. But even when we are overwhelmed, confused, and guilt-ridden, there is something we can all do to help—we can have a dialogue. One critical dimension of recovery is personhood. According to the aforementioned report on mental health recovery, personhood affects and is affected by the recovery process, personhood meaning "the internal sense of self, inner strivings," the "whole being (physical, emotional, mental, and spiritual)." Personhood is "about hope, purpose, faith, expectancy, respect and creating meaning." It is about "developing a sense of meaning, purpose and spirituality as well as having goals, options, role models, friends, optimism, and positive personal experiences [that] support recovery."[140] Perhaps personhood is the component of recovery that can be most impacted by intergenerational dialogue.

Prevention is another aspect of mental health we tend to forget about, but we should focus on prevention strategies because they have been shown to prevent some mental health conditions. Prevention can also reduce the severity of symptoms or delay the onset of those symptoms. Some strategies are put in place to manage the environmental factors that scientists believe contribute to mental health, including "exposure to alcohol, illegal drugs, and tobacco; low birth weight; brain injury or oxygen deprivation; infection, poor nutrition, or exposure to toxins in the environment . . . ."[141] Other strategies seek to enhance behavioral health by improving the conditions where people work, play, and live; building connections and relationships; enhancing economic opportunities; and establishing educational programs that focus on the cognitive, problem-solving, and social skills of children and adolescents. Intergenerational dialogue can be easily integrated into an overall prevention program to effectively speak to many of these needs.

It grieves me to say that sometimes embracing recovery and prevention means that even when you have done everything you can to support someone, they may still refuse to take the journey of healing and transformation, or they may get lost along the way. If that is the case for you, please know I do not want my message to trivialize your efforts or increase your pain in any way. Mental illnesses like anxiety and depression are diseases, and the hard truth is that we cannot always save people, even those we love the most.

No act of kindness, no matter how small, is ever wasted.

— Aesop

CHAPTER 10

GUIDELINES FOR EFFECTIVE INTERGENERATIONAL DIALOGUE

My discovering my own identity doesn't mean that I work it out in isolation, but that I negotiate it through dialogue, partly overt, partly internal, with others.

— Charles Taylor, *Multiculturalism: Examining the Politics of Recognition*

I have always had a love and appreciation for language—the beauty of the sounds, the way carefully nuanced words and use over time alter meaning, how meaning is conveyed and then how it is understood or misunderstood. I am also drawn to the complexity of the brain—how we think; how we learn; how our environment, our social context, and technology impact the way we come to know, understand, and internalize meaning. And then there is the essential transmitter of both—communication. My exploration of language and thought will be a lifelong journey. But through the course of searching for answers to my son's anxiety and depression, I have developed a framework that I apply in my life and that you can use too.

I discovered that while it is good to know a person, to understand them is better. And while it is good to know ourselves, to understand ourselves is better. And the bridge to understanding ourselves, our children, and each other in this rapidly changing world that has so distanced the generations is communication. The interchange of ideas gives us context for discovery. Thus, intergenerational dialogue promises to go a long way in helping us repair the societal and spiritual disconnects and learn to live healthier, richer lives.

BENEFITS OF INTERGENERATIONAL DIALOGUE

The power of intergenerational dialogue is fivefold.

1. Intergenerational dialogue empowers us to answer big life questions.

I recently read this interesting quote from a psychologist: "It is a commonplace observation that 'everybody sees the world in his or her own way.' However trite, this truism conceals an ancient and profound insight, the implications of which have been but poorly grasped in contemporary psychology."[142] And, I would argue, poorly grasped by society as a whole. Everyone has a worldview, not "worldview" in the broad sense as in Christian worldview, naturalist worldview, or new age spirituality worldview, but "worldview" in the sense of the lens through which we perceive the world. It is this lens that gives shape to each of our belief systems—the way we view the nature of reality, how we comprehend the meaning of life, and how we understand the purpose of our existence. This lens not only affects our perception of the world around us, but also determines the nature of our relationships, the types of societies we create, the ways we approach science and religion, and the manner in which we deal with opportunities and challenges that we encounter in our lives. This lens affects every aspect of our lives and everything we do.[143]

Recently I was listening to a podcast of "Selected Shorts" that reminded me how important it is that we continuously inspect the lens and adjust the focus. It also impressed upon me the fact that we all need to continuously examine our lives, regardless of our age or generation. The topic of the podcast was "convergence," and Estelle Parsons read Flannery O'Connor's short story *Everything that Rises Must Converge*. Here is an excerpt in script format:

Julian's Mother: If you know who you are, you can go anywhere . . . I can be gracious to anybody. I know who I am.

Julian: They don't give a damn for your graciousness. Knowing who you are is good for one generation only. You haven't the foggiest idea where you stand now or who you are.

Julian's Mother: I most certainly do know who I am. And if you don't know who you are, I'm ashamed of you.

Julian: Oh hell.

Julian's Mother: Your great-grandfather was a former governor of this state, and your grandfather was a prosperous landowner. Your grandmother was a Godhigh.

Julian: Will you look around you and see where you are now? [indicates the dingy neighborhood]

Julian's Mother: You remain what you are. Your great-grandfather had a plantation and 200 slaves.

Julian: There are no more slaves.[144]

Julian's mother, wholly constrained by her unexamined lens, cannot adapt, and, in fact, does not survive. She collapses and dies shortly after this exchange. You see, we may know who we are based on our genes and our environment, but to look only through that lens is detrimental to our well-being. However, we shouldn't want Julian's mother to simply change her worldview for the sake of satisfying her son or accommodating a new era; in fact, we should discourage that kind of throwing away of convictions for the ease of conformity. Instead, we should want her to seek a renewed intellectual understanding of the world and a societal and spiritual connection that reaches beyond biological or demographic limits, to the place where answers to the big life questions ultimately lie. Likewise, we should want to go there, and we should want our children and grandchildren to go there, so we can ask the big life questions, which can radically enrich our life experience and give us a more solid foundation in a precarious world.

Let me also suggest that there are times we find ourselves at the opposite end of the spectrum. There we fall prey to the zeitgeist of the times and become complacent, meandering through life as if floating down the river. This insightful statement from an engineering professor examining his own worldview sums it up: "If you fail to be conscious of your worldview and fail to appeal to it as a basis for your thoughts and acts, you will be at the mercy of your emotions, your impulses, and your reflexes . . . you will be inclined to 'follow the crowd' and conform to social and cultural norms and patterns of thought and behavior regardless of their merit."[145] Living intentional lives gives us confidence to live every day fully and have peace in the end, content that we redeemed our time here on earth to the best of our ability. As the Scriptures say in Ephesians 5:15-16 KJV: "See then that ye walk circumspectly, not as fools, but as wise, redeeming the time, because the days are evil." Living intentional lives requires first that we manage our knowledge of the world around us—what we know, why we know it, and how we process and internalize what we know. That knowledge internalized becomes the lens through which we see the world that, in turn, shapes our belief system. It is upon that foundation that we live out each day in community with others—managing what we think about, what we do with our time, how we act, how we react, and how we interact—with conviction and ease.

Engaging in intergenerational dialogue enables the critical process of evaluating and re-evaluating the lens through which we perceive the world and gives us the motivation and framework for seeking answers to big life questions.

2. Intergenerational dialogue forces us outside of ourselves.

We all know it. Common sense tells us. We have to strike a balance between being too isolated from society and not being isolated enough. To live healthy lives, we need to be able to interact within communities, yet we also need to be comfortable spending time alone with our own thoughts. Postmodern culture makes it difficult to achieve this balance. Unmet, unrealistic expectations breed feelings of isolation and loneliness, and those feelings are exacerbated by the perception of the self as the center of the universe, which is only complicated by feelings of uncertainty as we compare identities carefully crafted for public display on social media. Pretty soon, it becomes difficult to see the world outside of our own reality, and that is isolating.

As parents, we try to help our children achieve this balance when they are young. To help our kids interact with others, we put them in team sports; to help them understand their place in a big world, we travel and expose them to different cultures; to demonstrate socioeconomic differences, we serve Thanksgiving dinner to the needy in local soup kitchens; and to show them religious perspectives, we send them on mission trips. To help our kids feel comfortable in their own skin, we help them discover what they are good at, and we encourage them to develop those skills; we praise their strengths and help find ways to accept and compensate for their weaknesses; and we educate them and find ways to broaden their horizons. But even when we do all the right things to instill a sense of community, empathy, and compassion, oftentimes the force of society still tips the scale in favor of isolation, self-absorption, and loneliness.

Mental illness takes isolation and loneliness to a whole new level. The symptoms, which often occur out of the blue, can be disturbing and confusing. From the inside looking out, something painful and cataclysmic is happening to you, but you cannot explain it; you cannot put it into words, and even if you could, no one would understand. From the outside looking in, the observer notices significant changes in behavior, and looks for a logical cause. No explanation is provided, so one is left alone to interpret the signs. Your first instinct is to associate the problem with something you can put your finger on, like excessive drug use, for example, or some kind of traumatic experience, like child neglect. And then, when everyone finally begins to suspect mental illness, fear sets in. There is an abundance of information out there, but mental illness is still shrouded in mystery. Ignorance breeds fear, and when fear prevails, those with mental health challenges are left feeling ostracized.

The difficulty the mentally ill have in connecting with people comes not only from external sources, but from internal sources as well. As the blogger known as EmoVoid explains in a post describing her own depression:

I don't want to talk about myself, because of the shame I feel about what my life has become. So I stay in my bedroom, alone, where I don't have to worry about fielding unanswerable questions. Instead, I sit here in isolation, helplessly watching the dying embers of my youth as the dreams I had for my life evaporate into black smoke. It's a vicious cycle.

To break through the isolation, she suggests that we avoid small talk. What people who are suffering from anxiety and depression might most appreciate is "having a meaningful conversation that's not about them." If you talk to them about substantive issues of mutual interest, you are more likely to engage them and break through the barrier of isolation.[146]

Engaging in intergenerational dialogue provides a vehicle to draw us out of the realm of isolation and recursive self-talk into an interpersonal, shared human experience, which can be infinitely more positive and productive.

3. Intergenerational dialogue encourages us to go deep.

It is not easy to go deep, especially now. People are not reading as much or as often outside of office hours, and our busy schedules suck up any downtime we might otherwise have to stop and reflect. And when we do read, we are typically reading via links and popups, not via books and works cited. We are reading and thinking horizontally, not vertically. Some of the reasons for the trend may have to do with the number and types of books young people are required to read in school. I have been surprised many times to hear graduates say they never read a book during college. And while I recall having to do many close reading exercises as early as junior high, it seems that close reading is a lost art now.

But much of the problem can also be attributed to technology. It is widely held by the scientific community that our understanding of all kinds of information is shaped by our physical interaction with that information. In 2010 Nicholas Carr wrote an intriguing book titled, *The Shallows: What the Internet Is Doing to Our Brains*, in which he argues that when we consume information in a different form, it changes the way we "use, experience, and even understand the content." For example, "The shift from paper to screen doesn't just change the way we navigate a piece of writing. It also influences the degree of attention we devote to it and the depth of our immersion in it."[147] It is like when you want to refer back to information in a book and you are able to find it only because you remember the side of the page it was on or how the words appeared on the page.

The National Center for Biotechnology Information reported other disturbing results recently: the average attention span dropped from twelve seconds in 2000 to 8.25 seconds in 2015; 17 percent of page views last less than four seconds, while those that last more than ten minutes average 4 percent; and viewers only read 28 percent of the 593 words on an average webpage.[148] While it is too early to consider this research conclusive, the findings do indicate that screen navigation and consistent use of the Internet impede reading comprehension, the ability to retain information, and the capacity to focus attention. There can be no doubt that technology is impacting the already fragmented state of the postmodern mind.

Even more disconcerting is the potential technology has for rewiring the brain. Because of the plasticity of our brains, synaptic connections change, so the brain has the ability to reprogram itself. As discussed earlier, the way we think, believe, and act is a result of our genes, our environment, and the way we live, and, Carr adds, "through the tools we use." Whether the tools stimulate brain changes through repeated physical actions (like playing the violin regularly stimulates growth in the area of the cortex that processes the signals from the hand used to press the strings) or through pure mental activity (like driving a cab for years stimulates the part of the brain that stores and manipulates spatial relationships), they make changes to neural circuitry.[149] I am not suggesting that we reject technology and regress; that would be silly, of course. What I am suggesting is that we interject balance in our lives by reading more, reflecting more, and by using dialogue to support and encourage those activities, and to reinforce positive ways of creating meaning.

Engaging in intergenerational dialogue that takes us beyond thinking and talking about the "what" in our lives (our conclusions in other words) to the more interesting and purposeful "why" and "how," forces us to go deep.

4. Intergenerational dialogue helps us formulate a more stable sense of self.

A young person's search for identity in the twenty-first century is sabotaged by an unlimited quantity of information and a vast array of options all of various levels of usefulness and quality and all readily available. Unfortunately, the tools designed to sort it all out are oftentimes in short supply. There are many reasons why this might be the case, and this book addresses a few. Regardless, hope is not lost. If you are the parent of a teen, you can still provide those boundaries. If your child is an emerging adult, or if you are a church leader or a supervisor who ministers or manages twentysomethings, I suggest a different approach—mentoring and coaching.

Mentoring and coaching techniques are typically used in the workplace to help employees develop as leaders and reach particular career goals. In terms of intergenerational dialogue, these techniques can be used to help young people establish specific boundaries they might be lacking in their lives so that they can have something to react against in order to formulate a better sense of self. In some cases, mentees react by changing their perspective. A dialogue can trigger a change in perspective, particularly when the learning involves "values, ideas, feelings, moral decisions, and such concepts as freedom, justice, love, labor, autonomy, commitment, and democracy."[150] Or, the opposite could be a true. A dialogue could serve to reinforce a mentee's perspective. Either way, the value lies in the power of intentional back-and-forth conversation to create a more permanent sense of self.

I say that the dialogue helps the mentee when, in fact, it works both ways. What is so interesting about dialogue is that it sets up a dynamic relationship between the mentor and mentee (or the coach and the coached) so that at any given moment, the roles can switch. Let me give you a personal example: Bryce and I frequently disagree. When we repeatedly revisit topics about which we strongly disagree, we are known to get to the point where we reject the other person's point of view immediately, without giving it much consideration. While this is not a good dialoguing practice, it happens.

What is interesting is that after we ponder a conversation like that for a few days, we sometimes come back and confess to having learned something new. I, for one, am quick to shut down repeated complaints about established, proven workplace processes. You have boomers like me in the workforce who are trained in business process management, and a newbie walks in the door of the company and decides to leapfrog processes 475 to 476 and eliminate steps nine through twelve, fourteen, and twenty-one. What the heck! Yet in my moments of pondering, I realize that young people of the Technology Age are likely to be the ones who can introduce more agile, streamlined ways of conducting business. And to disregard their ideas simply because they are inexperienced might mean we overlook good opportunities for innovation.

Early in our practice of dialoguing, Bryce found himself relenting to my position on the topic of limiting his use of technology in much the same way as I changed my position on millennials and workplace processes and procedures. When I questioned whether he had to be connected to his peers virtually all the time, particularly while I was trying to engage with him in conversation, he insisted that he was only trying to multitask and make good use of his time. Some days later, we met again, and Bryce admitted that after he watched a Vimeo video about millennials and intergenerational dialogue, he could see my point. The guest speaker explained that when millennials use digital devices while engaging with others, boomers find it offensive. Boomers believe this behavior indicates a lack of interest.[151] "I understand now," Bryce said, at which point he committed to spend more time "interacting in the real, 2D world and less time in the virtual, 3D world." From now on, he said, "I'm going to spend more time being in the moment and experiencing the here and now."

Engaging in intergenerational dialogue helps us learn about other people, what makes them tick and why, but in the end, it may be that we learn even more about ourselves.

5. Intergenerational dialogue helps us find common ground.

Two of the biggest challenges we face in dialoguing are first, resolving conflict, and second, finding topics of mutual interest. You can expect to encounter both, particularly if you are a millennial dialoguing with a boomer.

The conversation between the Baby Boomer Generation and the Millennial Generation is often one of conflict. A quick Internet search will prove that to be true. Take an article I read recently titled "The Baby Boomer Legacy: The Millennial Perspective." The writer makes a few positive points about the contributions boomers have made to improve the world of work. She appreciates boomers for "changing the way we approach work/life balance," for example, and for being "great salespeople because they are calm, cool and collected."[152] Unfortunately, many of the comments are negative. Below are a few examples:

On February 4, 2015 at 1:52 pm, John said:

What utter nonsense. The boomers are the ones clinging to old technology because they learned everything through rote memorization. Millennials can't get into the workplace because the boomers, having messed up just about everything they ever touched have now realised they screwed up their retirements as well and so they're just sticking around, taking up space.

Gen-X made the current technology landscape; we are the ones who started out as "loser geeks" in the 80's and became today's modern-day professionals who do the actual work between the waste of space boomers and the hopeless Millennials.

On February 2, 2015 at 12:33 pm, Oliver J. said:

My dad is the perfect example of a boomer; he knows very well that his generation put the whole planet on a downhill trajectory to global catastrophe, but he couldn't care less. All he cares about is to make his millions last all the way through his very long and very golden retirement.

On January 28, 2015 at 1:46 pm, TC said:

As a member of GenX, this article just makes clear once again it's mostly my generation that's doing the "real" work, cleaning up the messes made by the endlessly-self-aggrandizing Boomers (like our author) and their bratty kids the Millennials, while we barely get a mention.

Conflict is simply a difference of opinion regarding a position, an idea, or a concept. And when there is a difference of opinion, it does not take long for the conflict to become more about power than the actual issue at hand, particularly when we are passionate about the subject matter. There is nothing like a good conflict to get your adrenaline going, and while some people thrive on that adrenaline rush, most people would do practically anything to avoid it. Either way, it is important that we find constructive ways to resolve our differences respectfully. Granted, some arguments (like which football teams deserve to go to the playoffs) are not meant to be resolved; in fact, they act as bonding agents in our relationships. But others, particularly the ones that challenge our persona (the qualities that define us but that we cannot change, such as place of birth, parents, race, and so on), or the ones that call our underlying belief system and values into question, are worth the time and energy we need to invest. By taking conflict out of the public domain and into the domain of interpersonal dialogue, we take away many of the negative attitudes that prevent compromise and consensus so we can approach a difference of opinion more enthusiastically and open-mindedly. This is important because working through conflict can help us discover more about ourselves.[153]

Regarding the challenge to find topics of mutual interest, chances are that your dialogue partner is either a family member or a person you choose. Therefore, you are likely to have something in common to start the conversation. As you progress, you can use dialogue to explore similarities and differences in preference and opinion. The topics you initially select will differ depending on how well you know your dialogue partner. If you do not know them well, for example, you may want to begin with less controversial topics like art and music and later delve into the realm of concepts and ideas. To gain the most value from dialoguing, however, make sure to go into depth; delve into the hows and whys of what made you formulate your opinions because those are the details that reveal what make you who you are. If it becomes a struggle to find something in common, many people find it is easier to begin by working on an activity together and then building a dialogue from there.

Engaging in intergenerational dialogue helps us identify commonalities between ourselves and other people, our generation and other generations, our race and other races, people who hold our opinions and people whose opinions differ from ours, and so on, thereby changing our attitudes and enabling us to move more easily from conflict to consensus.

DIALOGUE GROUND RULES

Through improved intergenerational dialogue, we can learn to better share ideas and corroborate to resolve crucial problems, and millennials are open to the conversation. If we play our cards right, their successors (Generation Y) will be too. So as parents, guardians, mentors, and church leaders, we have the unique opportunity to share our wisdom and experiences with them and grow from their creativity and enthusiasm. I can attest, however, that the chasm between the boomers and millennials often seems insurmountable. Millennials love us, but we frustrate them; we love them but find them exasperating. If we are willing to open up a dialogue on their terms and thereby find a way to interact effectively, chances are we can find common ground where an informed dialogue can prove mutually supportive and beneficial. To this end, all participants need to:

- Maintain an attitude of learning and support—We all have something to learn and something to teach, so no matter how young or how old, let's be open to all things new and be eager to pass on things that are tried and true.
- Use a common vocabulary and appropriate communication channels—Some words may not mean the same thing to you as they do to your dialogue partner, or maybe some words are entirely new, so let's mean what we say and explain what we mean.

- Be honest and nonjudgmental—Every strong relationship is built on trust, so what may seem like an innocent white lie or a constructive criticism to you may impose more damage than you might think. Don't take the "let's be real" approach, but be discerning and loving instead.

- Take responsibility—The goal of dialogue is to guide, encourage, and enrich, but when things go wrong (and they will on occasion), avoid the natural human tendency to point fingers, cast blame, or spin. Instead, own up to those hurtful words or actions, or anything you may have said in error (yep, that might mean saying you're sorry). Also, be willing to say "I don't know" when necessary and take time to find the answers.

- Be vulnerable, but not too vulnerable—My husband and I are private people, so we have to make a point of opening up and sharing anecdotes that can encourage our dialogue partners. Maybe you are like us, or maybe you are like those people I have seen on Facebook who have the tendency to overshare. Either way, think about it, and work toward striking the right balance.

KEYS TO EFFECTIVE INTERGENERATIONAL DIALOGUE

Share stories

What happens is of little significance compared with the stories we tell ourselves about what happens. Events matter little, only stories of events affect us.

— Rabih Alameddine, *The Hakawati*

Inform don't persuade

The purpose of a storyteller is not to tell you how to think, but to give you questions to think upon.

— Brandon Sanderson, *The Way of Kings*

Be patient and persistent

You never know what's around the corner. It could be everything. Or it could be nothing. You keep putting one foot in front of the other, and then one day you look back and you've climbed a mountain.

— Tom Hiddleston, actor

Know when to have tough love

I later learned that butterflies are designed to experience the struggle of breaking out of a cocoon. It's all part of the metamorphosis. The process is supposed to be challenging—it's the only way the butterfly will be strong enough to fly with those wings.

To the casual observer, it seemed all wrong not to help him as he fought and rested and then fought again. It felt cruel to let him do it on his own. I was sure I was doing him a favor by helping. I was wrong. I disabled him. The greatest help I could be was to allow him the privilege of growing up. I intruded on that privilege. I was well-intentioned in my efforts—but I interrupted his growth. I had removed the struggle and dealt a death-blow to the butterfly.

— Tim Elmore, *Generation iY: Our Last Chance to Save Their Future*

Leave the psychoanalysis and SSRIs to the psychiatrists

Doctors and more precisely psychiatrists can prescribe medications based on your medical history and your precise symptoms and with the full knowledge of the effects they might cause. However even in these cases using medication is a temporary solution at best (and often a very expensive one) and actually finding the source of the problem with therapy is very much preferable.

— Theodoros Manfredi, PhD, "Dangers of Self-Medication," Healthguidance.org

CHAPTER 11
INUKSHUKS TO HOPE

"Hope" is the thing with feathers—
That perches in the soul—
And sings the tune without the words—
And never stops—at all—

And sweetest—in the Gale—is heard—
And sore must be the storm—
That could abash the little Bird
That kept so many warm—

I've heard it in the chilliest land—
And on the strangest Sea—
Yet, never, in Extremity,
It asked a crumb—of Me.

— Emily Dickinson, *The Complete Poems of Emily Dickinson*

n summary, we have 1) established that there is a problem, 2) reached a better understanding of the problem by looking at societal and spiritual disconnects, and 3) established the value of using intergenerational dialogue to help repair those disconnects. The critical next step is to establish the focus of the dialogue; by doing so, we significantly raise the probability of success in achieving the goals of enriching lives and improving mental and spiritual health.

The idea is that effective intergenerational dialogue focuses on attaining mutual understanding about those concepts that young people struggle with most in the busyness, confusion, and ambiguity of the postmodern world: reading and reflecting, relaxing and rejuvenating, being rational and realistic, planning and persevering, and lastly, seeking progress and not perfection. That does not mean that older generations already mastered these concepts; we have some wisdom and experience, but we also have work to do. However, the focus is on helping young people, particularly millennials and their generational successors, who need to filter out the noise to find mental and spiritual health.

Let me suggest that we look at the practice of intergenerational dialogue as a journey. This journey is plagued by inclement weather, so imagine that the journey takes place in the Arctic in the midst of a blizzard. In the whiteout conditions, we lose our sense of direction. Confused and disoriented, we are not sure how to proceed. Thousands of years ago, the Inuit people, who are native to the Arctic, found a practical solution. By laying heavy stones one on top of the other, they constructed inukshuks so tall that they can be seen projecting out of the snow from great distances. These stone monuments served as markers to guide other natives to prime hunting and fishing grounds. By the same token, together we build inukshuks through intergenerational dialogue to guide the way to life-enriching, life-sustaining truths.

Millennials are different. If you are not convinced by now, go out there and see for yourself—watch them, talk to them, interact. They are different, right? And they learn differently too. In fact, experts in education and training are beginning to look at game design to find ways to keep millennials engaged so they will invest as many hours in educational initiatives as they do in playing video games. The term people use for this technique is "gamification." Gartner defines the word as "the use of game mechanics and experience design to digitally engage and motivate people to achieve their goals."[154] If you explore the topic, you will find other forms of the word such as "gamefulness" and "gamified."

As we endeavor to dialogue with millennials, it would behoove us to consider what it is about the way games are designed that keeps players motivated. Essentially, games are "machines for producing fist-pump-worthy challenges," explains Sebastian Deterding, designer, researcher, and head of the Gamification Research Network. When you play a game, you focus on a single goal, and as the difficulty and variety of challenges grow, your skills grow too, so you never get bored or frustrated. Furthermore, everything you do during the course of a game enables you to progress. Instead of starting out with an A grade and losing points when you fail, in the gaming world, with each challenge, you accrue experience points that enable you to progress through levels. Another notable aspect of game design is that you receive continuous, formative feedback; "with experience points, levels, progress bars, collected 'loot,' a log of completed 'quests,' and so on, you always know exactly where you stand, and what you still have to do to get to your goals."[155]

Deterding goes on to explain how game structure impacts learning. Games, he says, are structured so that goals are nested within goals and each goal is more complex than the one before; the result is that "you always see the relevance of your goal, and that you always have a next goal just within reach of you." For example, "you don't learn to jump for the sake of learning to jump, but to cross that chasm before you." And because there are multiple ways from which you can choose to attain a goal, the gamer feels a sense of autonomy. Finally, when you play games, you are allowed to fail; in fact, with failure, you are encouraged to determine how you failed, reflect on why you failed, and then devise a new strategy going forward. Not only does that learning strategy enforce problem-solving skills, but it can also help eliminate stress, fear, and anxiety. [156]

Over time, we have come to recognize the power of using visual imagery to communicate information. Whether read on the page or on the screen, words are abstract. Visual images, on the other hand, are concrete, so the value of images is clear: "Visuals can decrease learning time, improve comprehension, enhance retrieval, and increase retention." [157] Edward Tufte is one expert who has gone a long way in demonstrating that fact. Over the past decades, Tufte has written four powerful books describing how to design visuals that clearly convey complex technical information while maintaining the honesty and integrity of the data. His sophisticated charts, maps, and drawings give detailed attention to the proper arrangement of images, numbers, and words on the page and how they can convey motion, process, mechanism, and cause and effect with elegance and beauty.

The digitization of information and the rise of information technology continue to change the way we produce and consume knowledge at all levels. Ask any marketing firm or ask any millennial, and they will tell you: minimize the word count and maximize the visuals. Thus, we have the rising popularity of the picture-only social networking platforms like Snapchat, and highly visual platforms like Tumblr. And infographics are all the rage as web designers and content developers try to simplify information and make it easier to consume. The fundamental differences between Tufte's work and that of an infographics designer are that data visualizations are objective and are created for the purpose of making data sets more accessible to any audience, whereas infographics are subjective and are created to tell a story to a specific audience.

I recently discovered an infographic that tells the story of infographics and provides thirteen reasons why our brains crave them. One is because people are visually wired: "almost 50% of your brain is involved in visual processing, 70% of all your sensory receptors are in the eyes, and we can get the sense of a visual scene in less than 1/10 of a second." Also, infographics counter the negative impact of information overload because they are "more engaging," " more accessible," "more persuasive," and "easier to recall."[158]

So enough words already. In the next few pages, I will use infographics to express what I mean by "Inukshuks to Hope."

READ & REFLECT

When we read, we prefer books in print, but as news junkies, we want information bites available anytime, anywhere, across devices. In fear of missing out (FOMO), we scan, skim, link, surf, and update status all day long.

THE *average American*

READS
○ 19 minutes per day

CONSUMES INFORMATION
○ 18 hours per day

THE *skills*

% of Americans Who Did NOT Read a Book During the Past Year

8	16	13	13	18	16	18	23	23
Gallup 1978	Gallup 1990	Gallup 1999	Gallup 2001	Gallup 2002	Gallup 2005	Pew 2011	Pew 2012	Pew 2014

1 in 4 Americans

Do Not Read

READING *benefits*

- ☐ Adds to Life Experience
- ☐ Reduces Stress
- ☐ Boosts Brain Power
- ☐ Instills Empathy
- ☐ Expands Vocabulary
- ☐ Improves Memory
- ☐ Strengthens Analytical Skills
- ☐ Improves Concentration
- ☐ Increases Brain Connectivity
- ☐ Makes You a Better Writer

We do not learn from experience … we learn from reflecting on experience.

–JOHN DEWEY

REFLECTION:

The intentional attempt to synthesize, abstract, and articulate key lessons taught by experience.

REFLECTION *benefits*

- · *Imagination & Creativity*
- · *Problem Solving*   · *Productivity*
- · *Confidence in Your Ability to Achieve*

Get Lost in a Good Book

Dig deep & reflect

REST & REJUVINATE

We equate success with achievement, and achievement with happiness. Oftentimes, stress, anxiety and depression, follow, and can physically interfere with the body's relaxation mechanisms.

– John Dewey

STRESS *stats*

HIGHEST LEVELS

- Parents of kids < 18
- Gen Xers
- Millennials

3 in 4 Americans

Are Stressed About Money

Stress Management Techniques Among Millennials

All Americans | Millennials w/ high $ stress | Millennials w/ low $ stress

	Watch TV/movies >2 hrs. per day	Surf the internet	Nap/sleep	Eat	Drink alcohol	Smoke
All Americans	40	38	46	41	14	12
Millennials w/ high $ stress	58	67	27	23	25	21
Millennials w/ low $ stress	35	35	24	19	9	3

?N? Qrpcqq ɡ ?k cpgt_ Pcnmp" Dc' ps_pv2° 0. / 3,

STUDIES *show*

Emotional support from family & friends lowers stress levels & encourages healthier stress management.

STRESS *how it works*

Automated Nervous System

Sympathetic Nervous System ———|——— Parasympathetic Nervous System

Stress Turns ON

Fight vs Flight Response Switch

Relaxation Turns OFF

Releases hormones, triggering 1400 bodily changes for strength & speed

Returns all hormones, organs, & systems back to pre-stress levels

The system is designed to work well occasionally. But when the postmodern world keeps flipping the switch, the buildup of stress hormones can have a negative impact.

Stress affects systems, organs, and tissues all over the body.

Go to stress.org/stress-effects for symptoms.

GOOD NEWS

You can influence how stress affects you!

Sometimes the most productive thing you can do is relax.

— MARK BLACK

 RELAXATION *benefits*

- *Lowers stroke risk*
- *Protects the heart*
- *Keeps you in the mood*
- *Helps keep you fit*
- *Eases acne/skin conditions*
- *Lowers risk of catching a cold*
- *Helps ward off depression*
- *Enables better decision making*
- *Slows progression of breast cancer*

Take joy in the little things; they're the best, & they're free!

Don't Feel Guilty About Relaxing

Be Rational & Realistic

While our cultural attitude toward our twenties has always been "something like good old American irrational exuberance," says Meg Jay in The Defining Decade, the cultural paradigms of the twenty-first century have elevated the level of unrealistic optimism, and thus the resulting naivety and devastation.

– Ambra Watkins
Escape from Dark Places

EDUCATION *stats*

% completing at least a bachelor's degree at age 18 to 33.

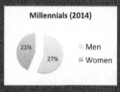
Millennials (2014)
21%
27%
Men
Women

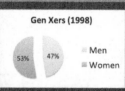
Gen Xers (1998)
53% 47%
Men
Women

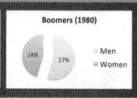
Boomers (1980)
14%
17%
Men
Women

Pew Research Center

PREPAREDNESS *stats*

51% Business Decision Makers who give recent college graduates a C grade or lower

66% Recent college graduates who say unpreparedness is a real problem among their own cohort

Bentley University

In a Survey of 23 Countries

 MILLENNIALS FALL SIGNIFICANTLY BEHIND IN:

▶ Literacy

▶ Practical Math

▶ Problem solving in technology-rich environments

ETS America's Skills Challenge

THE *Millennials*

 ## DEMOGRAPHICS

- The Largest Living Generation
- Makes Up 30% of the Workforce
- Makes Up 40% of Unemployed Workers
- The Most Underemployed Generation

"We are open-minded, creative, educated and diverse individuals with entrepreneurial spirits and a refusal to settle. We're tech-savvy and constantly connected, idealistic and adaptive. We have a drive for success, and although it might take us longer than previous generations to find it, it will be on our terms, because if we don't like our employment options, we create our own."

— bustle.com

POSTMODERN WORLD

- Amibiguous
- A Deluge of Information
- Hyperindividualistic
- Disconnected & Isolating
- Devoid of Meaning & Purpose

 Somehow, we need to either help these students become more realistic up front or better prepare them for the world that awaits them.

— TIM ELMORE

Actively Seek Understanding

Take action & prepare

STAY CALM & PERSEVERE

Even with factors like debt, negative cultural messages and a world full of dysfunctional institutions, for millennials, perseverance seems to be the primary challenge. When asked about what advice they would have for millennials striving to change the world today, the experts all answered the same: Don't give up.

– Jesse Carey, *RELEVANT* Magazine

THE *stats*

EMPLOYEES

- O >50% overwhelmed
- O 28% overworked
- O 29% no time to reflect on work

COLLEGE FRESHMEN

Fall	Frequently Depressed	Overwhelmed by Schoolwork
2009	6.1%	27.1%
2014	9.5%	34.6%

TEENS

Healthy	School Year	Summer
3.9	5.8	4.6

10 pt. scale

Teens underestimate the impact of stress on health.

Stress Symptoms

Irritable/Angry	37%
Nervous/Anxious	35%
Disinterested/Unmotivated	34%
Fatigued	32%
Depressed/Sad	32%
Overwhelmed	32%

?N? Qpcqq g ?k cpg_ Pcnmp' Dc' ps _pv2*0. / 3,

THE *message to:*

Employees

> We're in a recession. The business has to produce more with less.

College Students

> You're competing for jobs in a global market. Stay on your game.

> College admission is competitive. Do more. Work harder.

High School Students

MANAGE THE ANGST

CONTROL PERCEPTIONS

" *I always tried to turn every disaster into an opportunity.* "

— JOHN D. ROCKERFELLER

AIM HIGH

" *Say each to yourself. "My place is at the top." Be king in your dreams. Make your vow that you will reach that position, with untarnished reputation ...* "

— ANDREW CARNEGIE

SWEEP FLOORS

Humility is a valuable trait. As Andrew Carnegie once said, "It is well that young men should begin at the beginning," and that our first jobs often "introduce us to the broom."

Focus On Developing Who You Are

Photo © 2011 William Dustin Watkins

Start somewhere!

Work hard!

Don't quit!

Progress Not Perfection

Striving for excellence and setting unrealistic expectations for yourself are very different things. The former is actually ambition. The latter is a crippling condition, and it can be a dream-killer if you're not careful to cure it.

– Rebecca Strong

THE *definition*

Perfectionist: A person who refuses to accept any standard short of perfection

HEALTHY STRIVER	PERFECTIONIST
O Sets high goals/standards	O Sets unrealistic goals/standards
O Motivated by desire to excel	O Motivated by need to avoid failure
O Derives pleasure from striving & from succeeding	O Rarely derives pleasure from striving or succeeding
O Copes with stress	O Avoids stress

THE *stats*

Perfectionism

Linked to Depression & Suicide

1:5 to 1:3
Students

 to

O High School
O College

Perfectionists

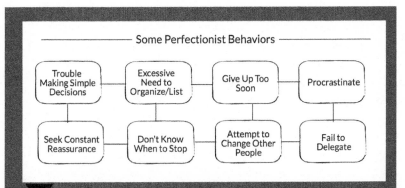

Some Perfectionist Behaviors

- Trouble Making Simple Decisions
- Excessive Need to Organize/List
- Give Up Too Soon
- Procrastinate
- Seek Constant Reassurance
- Don't Know When to Stop
- Attempt to Change Other People
- Fail to Delegate

DON'T *measure self-worth by:*

   Accomplishments

Productivity

What others think

SELF-WORTH IS:

Your Value as a Human Being

The greatest mistake we make is living in constant fear that we will make one.

– JOHN MAXWELL

Focus on Solutions

Be Flexible

Ask for help!

CONCLUSION

The world is indeed full of peril, and in it there are many dark places; but still there is much that is fair, and though in all lands love is now mingled with grief, it grows perhaps the greater.
— J.R.R. Tolkien, *The Fellowship of the Ring*

S o I raised my kids the best I knew how, as the majority of us did. Sometimes I parented with my heart when I should have parented with my head, but my children's happiness and safety were always the top priority. I tried to raise them with just the right combination of unconditional love and mercy mixed with tough love and justice. I fed them and clothed them, and I comforted them when they were hurt or sad. And I played with them and read to them and taught them how to count and read. But I had little control over their environment. I couldn't stop the evolution of the postmodern mindset.

I could try and influence but could not choose the core values and characteristics that came to embody my children's generations.

Over time, we lost some valuable traditions, like sitting on the front porch with grandparents and absorbing their more seasoned and experienced wisdom. Or gathering around the dinner table conversing about what it means to live in the world and to work and grow and raise families. This loss of tradition in combination with the massive change initiated by globalization and the information technology explosion was bound to cause disconnects—disconnects between the self and community, between the self and spirituality—but what surprises me most is the extent to which our children have lost their overall sense of self. I cannot change the evolution of thought or the fact that there is a gaping abyss between boomers and millennials, but I can build a bridge.

We can build a bridge through effective intergenerational dialogue. We can come to understand each other at a much deeper level in a way that will enrich everyone's lives. There is nothing to lose, and there is everything to gain. Through intergenerational dialogue, we can raise the awareness of mental illness, help prevent conditions such as stress, anxiety, and depression, and encourage those already affected by mental illness as they journey along their path to recovery. Through intergenerational dialogue, we can inspire all young people to examine how they perceive the world and consider whether there are healthier ways to live in relationship with God and with community.

THE POWER OF INTERGENERATIONAL DIALOGUE

Escape from Darkness is a call to action that provides the background and framework for change. If you recall from the personal journey I described in Chapter 1, the reality of anxiety and depression did not strike home immediately. It kind of slithered in through a crack in the foundation, raising its head only long enough to make us suspicious of its presence. It was not until the venom had reached critical levels that we were able to acknowledge the damage and start mitigating future risk. Not that we immediately knew what kind of snake we were up against. First we had to decompress and diagnose. Then we were able to start a dialogue. Through the dialogue, we were all able to learn and grow. Most importantly, Bryce found the hope he needed to start the healing process and the ongoing support he needs to persist in his journey toward happiness and success. We choose to share our search for answers to a millennial's anxiety and depression because it is the right thing to do.

A FINAL THOUGHT

In my dialogue with Bryce, I learned what it means to have anxiety and depression *and* what it means to love somebody who is suffering. It is painful to take the journey, and it is painful to watch someone you love struggle. But regardless of how bad it got, I always knew the big-hearted Bryce of the past lay just under the surface of the anger and frustration and just beyond the cloud of sadness. I remember seeing glimpses of it in the long string of conversations that led back to that graduation day. The young man who barely had the wherewithal to lift his head off of his pillow is now pursuing a job opportunity in New York City—an open-ended opportunity that offers neither tranquility nor security, but an opportunity for Bryce to do something he has always wanted to do and to discover more about himself. I think this excerpt from a recent email to family will give you a sense of his strength and a glimpse of his heart too:

> *First and foremost, I want to start off by saying that I'm sorry. I know I've been driving you guys up a wall with questions, seeking constant advice about New York. I can't express to you more about how much I love each one of you. I'm going to continue to grind it out here in New York for a year. My goal is to grow up and this*

is a lifetime opportunity to do just that. I know all of the risks, I know there will be stress, and I know that I will need perseverance to make this decision work. I know this is the only way to grow up. I can't stomp my feet and get my way . . . because there are six million people here that are here for the same reason I am—to build a better future.

Love you all very much

ABOUT THE AUTHOR

 Ambra Watkins, the mother of multiple millennials, is intrigued by what is proving to be a baffling yet compelling generation. She is concerned for trophy kids whose high expectations crashed into the reality of an economic downturn and is burdened for those souls that are desperately searching for meaning and purpose in the ambiguity of the postmodern world.

Ambra holds a master's degree in rhetoric and writing and a Project Management Professional (PMP) Certification. She worked for more than fifteen years designing, developing, and implementing large training, knowledge management, and organizational change initiatives at Accenture and other Fortune 500 companies. Her experiences living and working in northern Africa and traveling extensively in Europe, South America, and the Middle East lend a multi-cultural perspective to her life and her writing.

Other publications include a book detailing the story of a 123-year-old textile mill at the historical center of a small New England town—*The Birth, Being and Burning of Worumbo Mill*—as well as two self-published biographies that capture the values and character of the past through the lives of G.I. Generation women. Ambra has also contributed more than twenty-five articles to various newspapers and magazines including *Yankee Magazine, Lewiston Sun Journal, Times Daily,* and *RiverViews* magazine.

Ambra lives in Denver, Colorado, where she and her husband enjoy a view of the mountain ranges and spend downtime hiking, biking, snowshoeing, and skiing. Ambra is pursuing her goal of becoming a full-time author and working to establish Guideposts to Hope, Inc., to provide tools that will empower young people to find purpose and hope in the postmodern Age of Anxiety.

Connect with Ambra to share your stories and learn more about intergenerational dialogue:

- Website: http://www.ambrawatkins.org
- Email: ambra@ambrawatkins.org
- Twitter: https://twitter.com/AmbraWatkins, #inukshuk
- Facebook: https://www.facebook.com/guidepoststohope
- Google+: https://plus.google.com/+AmbraWatkins
- LinkedIn: https://www.linkedin.com/in/ambrawatkins
- https://www.youtube.com/c/AmbraWatkins

NOTES

CHAPTER 3

1   Robert Burton, *The Anatomy of Melancholy*, vol 1. 11th ed. (London, England: Thomas Tegg, Cheapside, 1845), 253.

2   Scott Stossel, *My Age of Anxiety: Fear, Hope, Dread, and the Search for Peace of Mind* (New York: Alfred A. Knopf, 2013), iBooks, chap. 4.

3   "Anxiety Drugs: The Facts about the Effects," Citizens Commission on Human Rights (2008), accessed June 8, 2015, http://www.cchr.org/sites/default/files/education/anti-anxiety-booklet.pdf.

4   Stossel, *Age of Anxiety*, chap. 1.

CHAPTER 4

5   "Stress in America™: Missing the Healthcare Connection," American Psychological Association (February 7, 2013), accessed November 18, 2014, https://www.apa.org/news/press/releases/stress/2012/full-report.pdf.

6   "American Psychological Association Survey Shows Teen Stress
        Rivals That of Adults," American Psychological Association
        (February 11, 2014), accessed June 25, 2014, http://www.apa.
        org/news/press/releases/2014/02/teen-stress.aspx.

7   "Stress: The Different Kinds of Stress," American Psychological
        Association, accessed November 12, 2014, http://www.apa.org/
        helpcenter/stress-kinds.aspx.

8   Rollo May, "Toward an Understanding of Anxiety," *Pastoral
        Psychology*, March 1950, 26.

9   Meg Jay, PhD, *The Defining Decade: Why Your Twenties Matter
        and How to Make the Most of Them* (New York: Twelve, 2012),
        iBooks, "Being in Like."

10   "Chronic Stress Puts Your Health at Risk," The Mayo Clinic
        (July 11, 2013), accessed October 20, 2014, http://www.
        mayoclinic.org/healthy-living/stress-management/in-depth/
        stress/art-20046037.

11   Jackie Burrell, "College and Teen Suicide Statistics: The Grim
        Numbers Behind Adolescent Suicides and Attempts," *About
        Parenting*, accessed October 24, 2014, http://youngadults.about.
        com/od/healthandsafety/qt/suicide.htm.

12   "Learn about the Issue," National Alliance on Mental Illness,
        accessed July 6, 2015, http://www2.nami.org/Content/
        NavigationMenu/Find_Support/NAMI_on_Campus1/Learn_
        About_The_Issue/Learn_About_The_Issue.htm.

13   Michael Kerr and George Krucik, MD, accessed June 23, 2014,
        "Depression and College Students," Healthline Networks,
        March 29, 2012, http://www.healthline.com/health/depression/
        college-students.

14   "American College Health Association-National College Health
        Assessment II: Reference Group Executive Summary Spring
        2012," Retrieved from http://www.acha-ncha.org/docs/ACHA-

NCHA-II_ReferenceGroup_ExecutiveSummary_Spring2012. pdf, 5.

15 Robert Gallagher, "National Survey of College Counseling Centers 2013 Section One: 4-Year Directors," The International Association of Counseling Services, Inc., 4.

16 "American College Health Association-National College Health Assessment II," 14.

17 S.E. McCabe, B.T. West, and H. Wechsler, 2007, "Trends and college-level characteristics associated with the non-medical use of prescription drugs among US college students from 1993 to 2001," accessed June 25, 2014, Addiction 102, no. 3: 455-465, CINAHL with Full Text, EBSCOhost.

18 Rebecca A. Vidourek, Keith A. King, and Ellen E. Knopf, "Non-medical Prescription Drug Use Among University Students," *American Journal of Health Education* 41, no. 6, (November/December 2010): 345-352.

19 "Nonmedical Use of Prescription Stimulants," The Center on Young Adult Health and Development, University of Maryland, accessed June 24, 2014, http://medicineabuseproject.org/assets/documents/NPSFactSheet.pdf?utm_source=Red+Alert-Prescription+Drugs&utm_campaign=Teens+Under+Stress&utm_medium=email, 2.

20 Denise Mann, "Illegal Drug Use on the Rise in US," WebMD, accessed June 23, 2014, http://www.webmd.com/mental-health/addiction/news/20110908/illegal-drug-use-on-the-rise-in-the-us.

21 Patrick Kennedy, *The Colbert Report* (Feb. 10, 2014), accessed July 13, 2014, http://thecolbertreport.cc.com/videos/hmu6hf/patrick-kennedy.

22 Margarita Tartakovsky, MS, "Depression and Anxiety among College Students," Psyche Central, last reviewed Jan. 30, 2013,

accessed Oct. 22, 2014, http://www.acha-ncha.org/data/
PHYSMENTALF06.html.

23 Melissa Thompson, "Let's End the Stigma of Mental Illness,"
updated Sept. 1, 2013, http://www.huffingtonpost.com/melissa-
thompson/lets-end-the-stigma-of-mental-illness_b_3522563.
html.

24 "The Effects of Adderall," DrugAbuse.com, accessed June 25,
2014, http://drugabuse.com/library/the-effects-of-adderall-use.

25 "The Truth about Prescription Drug Abuse," Foundation for
a Drug-Free World, accessed June 25, 2014, http://www.
drugfreeworld.org/drugfacts/prescription/depressants.html.

26 "What Are the Effects of Opioid Abuse and Addiction?"
Healthline Networks, accessed June 25, 2014, http://www.
healthline.com/health/opioids-and-related-disorders#Effects2.

27 Vidourek, King, and Knopf, "Non-medical Prescription Drug
Use," 348.

28 Sharon Jayson, "Teens feeling stressed, and many not managing
it well," *USA Today* (February 14, 2014), accessed Nov. 12,
2014, http://www.usatoday.com/story/news/nation/2014/02/11/
stress-teens-psychological/5266739/.

29 Stossel, *Age of Anxiety,* chap. 1.

CHAPTER 5

30 David F. Wells, *The Courage to Be Protestant: Truth-Lovers,
Marketers, and Emergents in the Postmodern World* (Grand
Rapids: Eerdmans, 2008), 61.

31 Paul Taylor, *The Next America: Boomers, Millennials, and the
Looming Generational Showdown* (New York: Public Affairs,
2014), iBooks, preface and intro.

32 Wells, *Courage to Be,* 142.

33   David F. Wells, "The Rejection of the Classical Doctrine of God," accessed March 27, 2014, http://www.monergism.com/thethreshold/articles/onsite/rejection.html, 3.

34   Mary Klages, PhD, "Postmodernism," accessed March 31, 2015, http://www.bdavential.com/Postmodernism.html, 2.

35   Ibid., 4.

36   Ibid.

37   Wells, *Courage to Be*, 63-67.

38   Lauren D. LaPorta, MD, "Twitter and YouTube: Unexpected Consequences of the Self-Esteem Movement?" *Psychiatric Times* (October 28, 2009), accessed June 12, 2015, http://www.psychiatrictimes.com/articles/twitter-and-youtube-unexpected-consequences-self-esteem-movement.

39   Wells, *Courage to Be*, 67.

40   Dictionary.com. Dictionary.com Unabridged, Random House, Inc., accessed June 13, 2015, http://dictionary.reference.com/browse/self-esteem, s.v. "self-esteem."

41   *Encyclopedia of Children in History and Society*, accessed June 13, 2015, http://www.faqs.org/childhood/Re-So/Self-Esteem.html, s.v. "self-esteem."

42   Dr. Benjamin Spock, quoted in "New E-book Format of Dr. Spock's Baby and Child Care," The Dr. Spock Website for Parents, accessed June 13, 2015, http://www.drspock.net/education-media/dr-spocks-baby-and-child-care-in-e-book-format-for-the-first-time/.

43   Therese Oneill, "'Don't Think of Ugly People': How Parenting Advice Has Changed," *The Atlantic* (April 19, 2013), accessed June 19, 2015, http://www.theatlantic.com/health/archive/2013/04/dont-think-of-ugly-people-how-parenting-advice-has-changed/275108/.

44 "Spock at 65: Five Ideas That Changed American Parenting," *Time* (July 14, 2011), accessed June 13, 2015, http://healthland. time.com/2011/07/14/65-years-since-spock-five-ideas-that-changed-american-parenting/photo/baby-feet-mom-hands/.

45 *Encyclopedia*, "self-esteem."

46 LaPorta, "Twitter and YouTube," 3.

47 Elisabeth Nesbit Sbanotto, PhD, (Psychotherapist and Assistant Professor of Counseling, Denver Seminary), interviewed by author, Littleton, CO, April 6, 2015.

48 Jay, *Defining Decade*, intro.

49 Jean M. Twenge, PhD, *Generation Me (Revised & Updated): Why Today's Young Americans are More Confident, Assertive, Entitled—and More Miserable than Ever Before*, (New York: Atria Books, 2014), chap. 4.

50 Ibid.

51 Nicole Kemp, "Why social media is constructing a reality unworthy of your anxiety," The Brand Republic Group (July 24, 2014), accessed October 24, 2014, http://www. marketingmagazine.co.uk/article/1305632/why-social-media-constructing-reality-unworthy-anxiety.

52 James Emery White, *The Rise of the Nones: Understanding and Reaching the Religiously Unaffiliated* (Grand Rapids, MI: Baker Books, 2014), iBooks, chap. 5.

53 Taylor, *Next America*, intro.

54 David Kinnaman, *You Lost Me* (Grand Rapids, MI: Baker Books, 2011), iBooks, chap. 1.

55 "Why Millennials Are Leaving the Church," YouTube video, 6:48, posted by JesusSavesAtCitiBank (August 18, 2013), accessed August 4, 2014, http://religion.blogs.cnn. com/2013/07/27/why-millennials-are-leaving-the-church/.

56   G.K. Chesterton, "The Ballad of the White Horse," Penn State
      University Electronic Classic Series, accessed July 14, 2014,
      http://www2.hn.psu.edu/faculty/jmanis/gkchesterton/Ballad-
      White-Horse.pdf.
57   Taylor, *Next America*, intro.
58   Ibid., chap. 4.
59   Ibid., chap. 2.

CHAPTER 6

60   "Turnings in History," Life Course Associates, accessed August
      2, 2014, http://www.lifecourse.com/assets/files/turnings_in_
      history(1).pdf, 3.
61   "Generational Archetypes," Life Course Associates, accessed June
      8, 2015, http://www.lifecourse.com/about/method/generational-
      archetypes.html.
62   Twenge, *Generation Me*, preface.
63   Jean M. Twenge, PhD, "A 'Greatest' Generation: Linking
      Personality, Eras," interview by Alix Speigel, NPR Author
      Interviews (May 18, 2006), accessed May 5, 2014, http://www.
      npr.org/templates/story/story.php?storyId=5415070.
64   Twenge, *Generation Me*, chap. 9.
65   Jean Twenge, PhD, "Generational Differences in Young Adults'
      Life Goals, Concern for Others, and Civic Orientation, 1966-
      2009," *Journal of Personality and Social Psychology* 102, no. 5
      (2012): 1,045-1,062.
66   Twenge, *Generation Me*, chap. 2.
67   Ibid., chap. 9.
68   Jeffrey Jensen Arnett, PhD, "Emerging Adulthood: A Theory
      of Development from the Late Teens through the Twenties,"
      American Psychologist 55, no. 5 (2000): 469.

69   Jeffery Jensen Arnett, PhD, *Emerging Adulthood: The Winding Road from the Late Teens through the Twenties*, 2nd ed. (New York: Oxford, 2014), iBooks, preface.

70   "The Barna Millennial Project," Barna Group, accessed March 11, 2015, https://www.barna.org/barna-update/millennials.

71   The Pew Research Center, accessed March 11, 2015, http://www.pewresearch.org/about/.

72   Taylor, *Next America*, intro.

73   Ibid., chap. 13.

CHAPTER 7

74   "What is a Generation?" LifeCourse Associates, accessed May 12, 2014, http://www.lifecourse.com/about/method/phases.html.

75   "The Boomers: Forever Young," *America's Generations with Chuck Underwood*, PBS, Sept. 23, 2015.

76   Hugh Rawson, "Why Do We Say 'G.I.'?" AmericanHeritage.com, accessed May 15, 2014, http://web.archive.org/web/20080829172935/http://americanheritage.com/articles/magazine/ah/2006/2/2006_2_15.shtml.

77   Ihn, trans., "General Eisenhower of Kansas," *The Kansas Historical Quarterly* 13, no. 7 (1945): 386, https://www.kshs.org/p/general-eisenhower-of-kansas/13002.

78   "America at the Turn of the Century: A Look at the Historical Context," Last Days of a President: Films of McKinley and the Pan-American Exposition, 1901 Collection, Library of Congress, accessed July 5, 2015, http://www.loc.gov/collection/mckinley-and-the-pan-american-expo-films-1901/articles-and-essays/america-at-the-turn-of-the-century-a-look-at-the-historical-context/.

79 Allison McNeill, Richard C. Hanes, and Sharon M. Hanes, eds. "Causes of the Great Depression," *Great Depression and the New Deal Reference Library*, Vol. 1: Almanac. Detroit: UXL, 2003, 1-20, U.S. History in Context, accessed June 28, 2015, http://ic.galegroup.com/ic/uhic/ReferenceDetailsPage/ ReferenceDetailsWindow?displayGroupName=Reference&zid =6d3bef0712b41d824dc3a746da70ef24&action=2& documentId=GALE%7CCX3425600011&userGroupName= mlin_c_montytech&jsid=c9674adb2ee4f7742f7c0575588b 0c0d, 4, 6.

80 McNeill et al, "Causes," 14.

81 Neenah Ellis, "Survivors of the Great Depression Tell Their Stories," *All Things Considered*, NPR (November 27, 2008), accessed July 2, 2015, http://www.npr.org/templates/story/story. php?storyId=97468008.

82 Studs Terkel, *Hard Times: An Oral History of the Great Depression* (New York: The New Press, 2005), iBooks, "A Personal Memoir."

83 Ibid., "A View of the Wood."

84 Ibid., "Concerning the New Deal."

85 William Manchester, *The Glory and the Dream: A Narrative History of America, 1932-1972* (New York: Little, Brown and Company, 1973), iBooks, "A House Divided."

86 Bob Henger and Jan Henger, *The Silent Generation: 1925-1945* (Bloomington: AuthorHouse, 2012), section 1.

87 Greg Knight, "The Suburbanization of America: The Rise of the Patio Culture," accessed July 13, 2014, http://www.patioculture. net/paper.html.

88 Bill Ganzel, "Farming in the 1950s & 60s," Wessel's Living History Farm, The Ganzel Group Communications, accessed July 13, 2014, http://www.livinghistoryfarm.org/ farminginthe50s/life_17.html.

89   Ronald J. Oakley, *God's Country: America in the Fifties* (New York: W.W. Norton, 1986), 239.

90   "Protests in the 1960s," accessed July 9, 2015, http://www.lessonsite.com/ArchivePages/HistoryOfTheWorld/Lesson31/Protests60s.htm.

91   "Flower Power," ushistory.org, accessed July 8, 2015, http://www.ushistory.org/us/57h.asp.

92   "Generation Jones," *Newsweek* excerpt, accessed March 25, 2016, http://www.generationjones.com/?jw_portfolio=newsweek.

93   Richard Fry, "Millennials surpass Gen Xers as the largest generation in U.S. labor force," Pew Research, May, 11, 2015, accessed July 29, 2015, http://www.pewresearch.org/fact-tank/2015/05/11/millennials-surpass-gen-xers-as-the-largest-generation-in-u-s-labor-force/.

94   Philip Martin and Elizabeth Midgley, "Population Bulletin Update: Immigration in America 2010," Population Reference Bureau (June 2010), accessed July 9, 2015, http://www.prb.org/Publications/Reports/2010/immigrationupdate1.aspx.

95   The Council of Economic Advisers, "15 Economic Facts About Millennials," October 2014, accessed July 29, 2015, https://www.whitehouse.gov/sites/default/files/docs/millennials_report.pdf, 6.

96   David F. Wells, *The Courage to Be Protestant: Truth-Lovers, Marketers, and Emergents in the Postmodern World* (Grand Rapids: Eerdmans, 2008), 71.

97   Twenge, *Generation Me*, intro.

98   David Gutierrez, "Helicopter parenting hurts children's mental health, study finds," *Natural News*, accessed May 17, 2014, http://www.naturalnews.com/039119_helicopter_parenting_children_mental_health.html#ixzz31W6hYKk8.http://www.

naturalnews.com/039119_helicopter_parenting_children_
mental_health.html#ixzz31W6hYKk8.

99 Jay, *Defining Decade*, intro.

100 Anne Fisher, "American Millennials Are Among the World's
Least Skilled," *Fortune* (March 10, 2015), accessed March 15,
2015, http://linkis.com/fortune.com/2015/03/0CSKO.

101 Andrea Caumont, "What would you name today's youngest
generation of Americans?" PewResearchCenter.org (March 12,
2014), accessed May 11, 2014, http://www.pewresearch.org/
fact-tank/2014/03/12/what-would-you-name-todays-youngest-
generation-of-americans/.

102 "2018 List," Beloit College, accessed July 5, 2015, https://www.
beloit.edu/mindset/2018/.

103 Tom McBride and Ron Nief, *The Mindset Lists of American
History: From Typewriters to Text Messages, What Ten Generations
of Americans Think Is Normal* (Hoboken, NJ: John Wiley &
Sons, 2011), iBooks, chap. 10.

CHAPTER 8

104 Wells, *Courage to Be*, 67.

105 "What Most Influences the Self-Identity of Americans?" Barna
Group, accessed May 18, 2015, https://www.barna.org/barna-
update/culture/712-what-most-influences-the-self-identity-of-
americans#.VVpTRmBaQs3.

106 Matt. 19:19, Matt. 22:39, Mark 12:31, Rom. 13:9, Gal. 5:14,
James 2:8.

107 Psalm 139:14, Gen. 1:27.

108 Wells, "Rejection," 5.

109 Søren Kierkegaard, *Fear and Trembling* (New York: Penguin,
1985), 66.

110 Ross Douthat, *Bad Religion: How We Became a Nation of Heretics* (New York: Free Press, 2012), 214-215.

111 Peter Kreeft, *The Modern Scholar: Faith and Reason: The Philosophy of Religion* (Recorded Books, 2005), audio book.

112 Søren Kierkegaard, Public Theology, accessed June 17, 2015, http://www.pubtheo.com/page.asp?pid=1010.

113 Francis Spufford, *Unapologetic: Why, Despite Everything, Christianity Can Still Make Surprising Emotional Sense* (New York: HarperCollins, 2013), iBooks, chap. 1.

114 "America's Changing Religious Landscape," Pew Research Center (May 12, 2015), accessed May 19, 2015, http://www.pewforum.org/2015/05/12/americas-changing-religious-landscape/#fn-23198-1.

115 Spufford, *Unapologetic*, preface to the US Edition.

116 Frank Newport, "Seven in 10 Americans Are Very or Moderately Religious," Gallup (December 4, 2012), accessed May 28, 2015, http://www.gallup.com/poll/159050/seven-americans-moderately-religious.aspx?utm_source=number%20of%20Americans%20who%20go%20to%20church%20regularly&utm_medium=search&utm_campaign=tiles.

117 Michael Paulson, "Americans Claim to Attend Church Much More Than They Do," *The New York Times* (May 17, 2014), accessed May 19, 2015, http://www.nytimes.com/2014/05/18/upshot/americans-claim-to-attend-church-much-more-than-they-do.html?abt=0002&abg=1.

118 Wells, "Rejection," 1.

119 Toni Ridgaway, "Statistics Don't Tell the Whole Story When It Comes to Church Attendance," Church Leaders Lead Better Every Day, accessed May 20, 2015, http://www.churchleaders.com/pastors/pastor-articles/170739-statistics-don-t-tell-the-whole-story-when-it-comes-to-church-attendance.html.

120   Matt. 13:30.

121   "What Isn't Being Talked About in the Pew Study," *Come Reason's Apologetics Notes* (blog) (May 18, 2015), accessed May 19, 2015, buff.ly/1S6CgVQ.

122   Thom S. Rainer and Jess W. Rainer, *The Millennials: Connecting to America's Largest Generation* (Nashville: B&H Publishing Group, 2011), iBooks, chap. 11.

123   Rachel Held Evans, *Searching for Sunday* (Nashville: Nelson Books, 2015), iBooks, prologue.

124   Jonathan Aigner, "Dear Church: An open letter from one of those millennials you can't figure out," *Ponder Anew: Discussions about Worship for Thinking People* (blog) (May 13, 2015), accessed May 31, 2015, http://www.theologyinworship. com/2015/05/13/dear-church-an-open-letter-from-one-of-those-millennials-you-cant-figure-out/.

125   Rainer, *Millennials*, chap. 11.

126   David F. Wells, PhD, "The Word in the World" (March 27, 2014), accessed May 18, 2015, http://www.the-highway.com/ wordworld_Wells.html, 9.

127   Wells, "Rejection," 2.

128   Casting Crowns, "Jesus, Friend of Sinners," *Come to the Well*, Provident Label Group, 2011, https://www.castingcrowns.com/ music/lyrics/jesus-friend-sinners.

CHAPTER 9

129   Rebecca A. Clay, "Yes, recovery is possible," *Monitor on Psychology* (January 2012), accessed June 17, 2015, http:// www.nxtbook.com/nxtbooks/apa/monitor_201201/index. php?startid=52#/54, 54.

130   Steven J. Onken, PhD, Jeanne Dumont, PhD, Priscilla Ridgway, MSW, Douglas H. Dornan, MS, and Ruth O. Ralph, PhD,

"Mental Health Recovery: What Helps and What Hinders? A National Research Project for the Development of Recovery Facilitating System Performance Indicator," National Association of State Mental Health Program Directors (NASMHPD) and the National Technical Assistance Center for State Mental Health Planning (NTAC) (October 2002), accessed June 3, 2015, http://www.nasmhpd.org/docs/publications/archiveDocs/2002/MHSIPReport.pdf, viii.

131 "Recovery," National Alliance on Mental Illness, accessed June 11, 2015, http://www2.nami.org/Content/NavigationMenu/Find_Support/Consumer_Support/Recovery.htm.

132 Recovery to Practice E-News, accessed June 24, 2015, http://dsgonline.com/rtp/rtp_enewsletter/Enewsletter_Final_4_30_10.html.

133 Benedict Carey, "Expert on Mental Illness Reveals Her Own Fight," Lives Restored, *The New York Times* (June 23, 2011), accessed June 17, 2015, http://www.nytimes.com/2011/06/23/health/23lives.html?pagewanted=1&_r=4&hp.

134 Brandon Appelhans and Nancy Buschart, "Suffering Redeemed: Finding Purpose in the Pain of Mental Disorder," *Engage* 1, no. 1, (2013): 17.

135 The Kennedy Forum, accessed June 20, 2015, https://www.thekennedyforum.org.

136 The Jed Foundation, accessed June 20, 2015, https://www.jedfoundation.org.

137 Clay, "Yes, recovery," 52-55.

138 Matt, in discussion with the author, May 3, 2015.

139 Susan Blackmore, *Consciousness: A Brief Insight* (New York: Sterling Publishing, 2005), iBooks, chap. 1.

140 Onken et al., "Mental Health Recovery," 70.

141 "Facts about Prevention of Mental Illness," Mental Health Reporting, University of Washington School of Social Work, accessed June 21, 2013, https://depts.washington.edu/mhreport/ facts_prevention.php.

CHAPTER 10

142 Mark E. Koltko-Rivera, "The Psychology of Worldviews," *Review of General Psychology* 8, no. 1 (2004), accessed March 20, 2015, http://www.arabphilosophers.com/English/research/non-arabic/ non%20arabic%20research/Mark%20E.%20Koltko-Rivera/ the_psychology_of_worldviews.pdf, 3.

143 H.B. Danesh, *Education for Peace Curriculum Manual: A Conceptual and Practical Guide* (Vancouver: EFP Press, 2007), 31.

144 Flannery O'Connor, *Everything that Rises Must Converge*, performed by Estelle Parsons, Selected Shorts from PRI, July 31, 2014, accessed July 30, 2014, podcast audio.

145 Kenneth H. Funk, PhD., "What Is a Worldview?" accessed May 9, 2014, http://web.engr.oregonstate.edu/~funkk/Personal/ worldview.html.

146 EmoVoid, "Why Depression Can Make Small Talk Intolerable," blog post (April 8, 2015), accessed April 12, 2015, http://www. emovoid.com/?s=McDonalds.

147 Nicholas Carr, *The Shallows: What the Internet Is Doing to Our Brains* (New York: W.W. Norton & Company, 2010), 90.

148 "Attention Span Statistics," Statistic Brain Research Institute, accessed July 9, 2015, http://www.statisticbrain.com/attention-span-statistics/.

149 Carr, *Shallows*, 31-33.

150 Reinhard Stelter, PhD, "Third generation coaching: Reconstructing dialogues through collaborative practice and a

focus on values," *International Coaching Psychology Review* 9, no. 1 (2014): 52-53, *PsycINFO*, EBSCO*host,* accessed May 28, 2015.

151   Dr. Rick Langer and Dr. Tim Muehlhoff, "Millennials— Intergenerational Interactions," Lightshed Table Talk #1, accessed May 28, 2015, https://vimeo.com/104735876.

152   Ritika Puri, "The Baby Boomer Legacy: The Millennial Perspective" (January 21, 2015), accessed July 7, 2015, https:// www.workintelligent.ly/workstyle/demographics/2015-1-21- baby-boomer-legacy-millennials-perspective/.

153   Robert J. Chadwick, *Finding New Ground: Beyond Conflict to Consensus,* (Terrebonne, TN: One Tree Publishing Company, 2012), 33-60.

CHAPTER 11

154   Brian Burke, "Gartner Redefines Gamification" (April 4, 2014), accessed June 3, 2015, http://blogs.gartner.com/brian_ burke/2014/04/04/gartner-redefines-gamification/.

155   Sebastian Deterding, "Gameful Design for Learning," *Talent Development Magazine* (July 8, 2013), accessed June 3, 2015, https://www.td.org/Publications/Magazines/TD/TD- Archive/2013/07/Gameful-Design-for-Learning.

156   Ibid.

157   Haig Kouyoumdjian, PhD, "Learning through Visuals," *Psychology Today* (blog) (July 20, 2012), accessed June 21, 2015, https://www.psychologytoday.com/blog/get-psyched/201207/ learning-through-visuals.

158   "Thirteen Reasons Why Your Brain Craves Infographics," Neomam Studios, accessed July 30, 2015, http://neomam.com/ interactive/13reasons/.

CPSIA information can be obtained at www.ICGtesting.com
Printed in the USA
BVOW08s1112180516

448588BV00006B/142/P